PRAISE FOR *BRINGING UP THE BOSS*

"I only wish that *Bringing Up the Boss* had been around when I got my first promotion to manager. The tools in this book are accessible and easy-to-use—I immediately put them into practice on my own teams. This is required reading for first-time and senior managers."

> **—Fiona Greig, President, JP Morgan Chase Institute**

"In fast-growing start-ups, it's up to managers to help guide their teams through constant change. Yet there are also many first-time managers who are often thrust into leadership roles with very little training and are unprepared for the new responsibilities that they will face. Rachel Pacheco expertly helps new managers learn the ropes with bite-sized lessons on how to effectively manage, lead, and inspire through change, particularly in high-growth start-ups."

> **—Katherine Ryder, Founder & CEO, Maven Clinic**

"Behind any great organization are strong managers who can motivate and inspire their teams. Over the course of my career, I've realized that the ability to do so is not innate, but learned. *Bringing Up the Boss* helps new and established managers quickly gain these skills and immediately apply them to their day-to-day."

> **—Stephan Jacob, Cofounder & COO, Cotopaxi**

"Start-ups are inherently crazy. *Bringing Up the Boss* is a great guide to help make them a little more sane by focusing on what managers in these high-growth companies need to do to succeed."

> **—Andrew Savage, Founding Team & Head of Sustainability, Lime**

"The lessons in *Bringing Up the Boss* are not unique to start-ups. Managers and leaders in the nonprofit world have needed an accessible book like this for years. Any person in a position of management will gain new insights and wisdom from this book."

> **—Janet Dalziell, former International Director of People and Culture, Greenpeace**

"When I started Wellthy, I quickly realized how challenging—and crucial—it is to train up new managers in a fast-growing environment. *Bringing Up the Boss* is required reading for leaders and managers alike, and especially for a person managing in a fast-growing company."

—Lindsay Jurist-Rosner, Founder & CEO, Wellthy

"Over the course of my career, I've learned the key to any great ensemble is open communication and honest, thoughtful feedback. *Bringing Up the Boss* acts as my conductor's score—instructing me how to do both and so much more. It's full of easily digestible nuggets of wisdom for real-world application on and off the stage."

—Joseph Conyers, Bassist, The Philadelphia Orchestra & Faculty, The Juilliard School

"Whether you're managing dozens, a handful or just one employee, *Bringing Up the Boss* will help you sharpen the skills you need to build and maintain a strong, happy team."

—Erin Lowry, author of the three-part BROKE MILLENNIAL series

BRINGING UP THE BOSS

BRINGING UP
THE BOSS

PRACTICAL LESSONS FOR
NEW MANAGERS

RACHEL PACHECO

Matt Holt Books
An Imprint of BenBella Books, Inc.
Dallas, TX

BenBella Books, Inc.
10440 N. Central Expressway
Suite 800
Dallas, TX 75231
benbellabooks.com
Send feedback to feedback@benbellabooks.com

BenBella is a federally registered trademark.
Matt Holt and logo are trademarks of BenBella Books.

Printed in the United States of America
10 9 8 7 6 5 4 3 2 1

Library of Congress Control Number: 2021905263
ISBN 9781953295019 (print)
ISBN 9781953295408 (electronic)

Editing by Vy Tran
Copyediting by Ginny Glass
Proofreading by Lisa Story and Cape Cod Compositors, Inc.
Text design and composition by Katie Hollister
Cover design by Heather Butterfield
Printed by Lake Book Manufacturing

To my mom and dad.

Thanks for everything you've done to bring up this boss.

CONTENTS

Introduction 1

What Is Management, and Why Do I Need This Book? 5

PART I: MANAGING AN INDIVIDUAL

Performance 11

CHAPTER 1: Great Expectations 13

CHAPTER 2: Feedback Is Like Underwear: It's a Gift You Need,
Maybe Not One You Want 21

CHAPTER 3: Own It! (Your Development, That Is) 37

CHAPTER 4: The Coaching Playbook 43

CHAPTER 5: Managing Performance Anxiety 50

A Final Note on Performance 60

Motivation 62

CHAPTER 6: The Trifecta of Motivation: Achievement, Power, and Affiliation 64

CHAPTER 7: Goal Interrupted: The Good and the Bad of Setting Goals 71

CHAPTER 8: The Complications of Compensation 79

CHAPTER 9: The Heavyweight Title Fight 90

A Final Note on Motivation 99

Meaning 102

CHAPTER 10: Making Work Meaningful 105

CHAPTER 11: There's No Crying in Baseball 114

CHAPTER 12: Talk Is Not Cheap 123

CHAPTER 13: Beautiful Questions 131

A Final Note on Meaning 138

PART II: MANAGING A TEAM

Hiring and Firing 143

CHAPTER 14: Interviewing 101 145

CHAPTER 15: Why the Airport Test Stinks 154

CHAPTER 16: The New Kid on the Block 161

CHAPTER 17: Breaking Up Is Hard to Do 167

A Final Note on Hiring and Firing 177

Team Dynamics 180

CHAPTER 18: The TINO (Team in Name Only) 182

CHAPTER 19: Getting Your Team to Speak Up 190

CHAPTER 20: The Good Fight: Conflict and What to Do About It 199

CHAPTER 21: The Meeting Paradox: We Hate Going, but We Still Want
             to Be Invited 205

A Final Note on Team Dynamics 212

PART III: MANAGING YOURSELF

Managing Yourself 217

CHAPTER 22: Confidence and Vulnerability 219

CHAPTER 23: Power: Use It for Good, Not Evil 225

CHAPTER 24: Managing Up 232

CHAPTER 25: Should I Stay, or Should I Go? 240

A Final Note on Managing Yourself 246

APPENDIX

Expectation-Setting Template 249

Individual Development Plan Template 250

Powerful Coaching Questions 251

Performance Improvement Plan Template 252

Motivation Intake Form 253

Competency Matrix Template 254
Interview Process Template 255
Affinity Bias Exercise. 256
Behavioral Interview Questions 258
Onboarding Template. 260
Psychological Safety Team Assessment. 262
Team Norms Template. 263
Job Dimensions. 264

Notes. 265
Acknowledgments 283
About the Illustrations 285
About the Author 287

INTRODUCTION

A number of years ago, I joined a small and growing start-up as the chief people officer. During my first week of work, I had coffee with Sandy, an employee who had joined the company two years earlier when it was only five people.[1] She was poised, knowledgeable about the business, phenomenal at the work she was hired to do . . . and totally freaking out. Sandy came on board fresh out of college, and now two years in, she was managing four new employees, some older than she. Earlier that day, she'd received her first upward performance review from her team, and the jury was in: Sandy was a terrible manager. Over oat-milk lattes, Sandy read me the litany of sins she had committed as a manager—most of them unbeknownst to her.

But was this a surprise? Sandy didn't have any work experience outside of our company, and she definitely had never managed before. Moreover, Sandy didn't have a skilled manager managing *her,* so she didn't have anyone to emulate. And our little boot-strapped start-up didn't exactly have tons and tons of money to send Sandy to a fancy management training or run a whole bunch of internal training programs. Sandy was desperately trying to keep her head above water as a manager and absolutely suffering in doing so. And even worse, Sandy's team members were suffering as she staggered in the dark trying to manage them.

Sandy's challenge is not unique.

Often, we are put into positions of management—especially in small and growing organizations—before we're actually ready. Our organizations grow quickly, and we are expected to grow in our roles with just as much speed. We end up stumbling along and doing our best, but our best

1

may make our teams miserable. In the start-ups and other organizations I've worked for over the years, I've seen this cycle repeated over and over again: Top performer gets promoted to manager, has no idea what to do, team members become unhappy and leave, and the new manager becomes unhappy and feels terrible about themselves and their job.[2] Repeat cycle.

Being a manager is a huge responsibility. For better or worse, we play outsized roles in how our teams experience their days and their jobs. We have the power to help someone grow, develop, and thrive; we also have the power to overburden, confuse, and wreak havoc. Many of us have personally had the experience of a terrible boss. And many of us have left jobs—jobs that otherwise were fulfilling—because we've had a manager who was not just awful but also unbearable.

> **We have the power to help someone grow, develop, and thrive; we also have the power to overburden, confuse, and wreak havoc.**

For the last fifteen years in my coaching, advising, and teaching, I've collected stories, experiences, and challenges that new managers face. In particular, I've focused on new managers in small and growing organizations who don't have the resources of a large company. These organizations may not be able to train their managers, send their employees to courses, or hire fancy business-school graduates (not that a diploma from a business school means you're a great manager—trust me). From these stories and challenges, I've developed a set of tools and best practices to help make the new manager's job a little easier.

But in this endeavor, I've learned (unsurprisingly!) that folks outside of the business world also suffer from a whole bunch of bad bosses and often have access to even fewer tools to build their management muscles. While this book started as a love letter to new managers in start-ups, I've also included stories from lawyers, doctors, college administrators, government workers, and—my favorite—spouses about the management challenges that pop up in their unique settings.

I wrote this book during the spring and summer of 2020. I pitched the book two weeks after New York and many other cities fully shut down due to the COVID-19 pandemic. The first meeting with my publisher, Matt, was over Zoom during the height of the first surge in early April. Employees, managers, and organizations began grappling with the collision of their work and home lives in a way like never before. Weeks later, the murder of George Floyd and the following protests brought to light racial dynamics that organizations and managers finally began to openly reckon with.

Many friends and colleagues asked if I were going to include a chapter on virtual work, or one dedicated to racial equity given what was surrounding all of us during this time. But you'll see that there isn't a dedicated chapter on managing remotely or on building a diversity and inclusion strategy for your team. That's because this whole book is written through one simple lens: how to manage across divides. This lens encompasses how to manage across geographic or temporal space as well as how to manage across differences. For example, strategies on how to manage in a way that is anti-racist and anti-oppressive aren't bolted onto this book as an extra chapter. They're built into each management lesson. Being a great manager means building an anti-oppressive and inclusive approach to the way you manage your teams across *all* components of management. Similarly, managing a team that is geographically dispersed and, even more so, managing through the uncertainty that results from the economic and health instability of a pandemic is not a single chapter. Being a great manager is ensuring that no matter where our teams are—over the computer, over the phone, or in person—they are being managed well.

> **Being a great manager is ensuring that no matter where our teams are—over the computer, over the phone, or in person—they are being managed well.**

I hope you are able to use this book throughout your long management journey. As you will see, this book is less a novella and more a playbook. There will be some chapters that you can start using tomorrow. There will be other chapters that don't feel immediately relevant but that you'll come back to over time—for example, when you hire (or fire) your first team member or decide to promote a high performer. I hope this book becomes dog-eared, underlined, coffee stained, and passed around to other managers, colleagues, and friends who might also be struggling with the responsibility bestowed on them.

And though the responsibility of management is serious, the way I approach it is not. We're all human. We're all going to make mistakes as we manage. We all start out as terrible managers, but over time, we can grow into something great. The irreverence sprinkled throughout this book is to remind you that you will most definitely screw up—sometimes in hilarious ways. You'll probably screw up so much at some point that a team member of yours will quit. Or you'll be called a bad boss. This is to be expected.

So let's jump into the saddle of this rewarding, messy, frustrating, fulfilling, and, at times, infuriating world of being a boss. Without further ado, I'm excited to begin my humble role as your Virgil on the quest to great management.

WHAT IS MANAGEMENT, AND WHY DO I NEED THIS BOOK?

I have a lot of conversations with executives from start-ups that go something like this:

> **EXECUTIVE:** Our managers have no idea what they are doing. We need manager training.
> **ME:** Well, what specific parts of managing are they most struggling with?
> **EXECUTIVE:** Managing.

Executives and managers want to learn what it takes to be a successful manager in the same ways that they learned how to program, how to design, and how to operate. They want something practical, something concrete, something they can use with their teams as quickly as possible. Perhaps they view learning to manage as a series of steps or tips that they can learn at a webinar or weekend management training. Simple, right? Well, not really.

It's hard to learn to manage. The first reason is because management is a whole bunch of things. Managing is knowing how and when to have difficult conversations. Managing is structuring work and breaking down problems. Managing is setting clear expectations. Managing is developing an individual's skills. Managing is giving critical and constructive feedback. Managing is motivating and incentivizing . . . The list goes on and on and on.

WE SAY, "TEACH ME THIS!"

MANAGEMENT

WHAT WE MEAN IS, "TEACH ME ALL OF THESE THINGS"

MANAGEMENT

In this book, I break management down into three main buckets: managing an individual, managing a team, and managing yourself.

In part one, **Managing an Individual**, we'll cover three main areas:

- **Performance**: how to ensure that your team member has the skills, feedback, and guidance to effectively do their job. *Think: How do I tell my team member that they are doing a downright stinky job on a project?*

- **Motivation:** how to ensure that your team member is driven and inspired by their role. *Think: Will my team member ever be happy with how much they are paid?*

- **Meaning**: how you structure the work and role of your team member to ensure that they find meaning and fulfillment in their job and career. *Think: What do I do when my team member asks, "Is this job fulfilling my life's purpose?"*

In part two, **Managing a Team**, we'll look at two primary areas:

- **Hiring and Firing:** how to hire, recruit, onboard, and exit team members. *Think: Holy moly, I have to fire someone, and I have no idea how.*

- **Team Dynamics:** how to help your team build a great culture, make effective decisions, and operate as a group. *Think: My team makes crazy decisions. Why?*

And in the final section, **Managing Yourself**, we'll discuss:

- **Your Approach as a Manager:** how you build and maintain the emotional fortitude to be a great manager, and how you think about your own career. *Think: What do I do when everyone hates me because I'm their boss?*

- **Your Relationship to Your Boss**: how to effectively manage your manager. *Think: How do I work with a boss that drives me bananas?*

We won't go over every single area you will need to understand in order to be a great manager, but we'll cover the most important ones. This book will give you a strong foundation for great management.

Now you know that management involves many different components that we will explore in this book. But there is another reason why learning how to manage is hard, and that's the challenge of time. At this point in your career, you are probably great at learning things. You've learned how to do your job well, and you've possibly been promoted a number of times. But learning how to manage people is not like learning how to code or learning how to build a marketing segmentation or learning how to write a great legal brief.

That's because you are likely facing a tension. Your organization is growing quickly, and you might be struggling to keep up with that growth. And learning how to manage takes time and just lots of practice. But often in fast-growing organizations, you don't have the luxury of time or repetitions. This book is structured to help you become aware of and practice these management skills as quickly as possible.

In each chapter, we'll talk about a management behavior that is critical to great management. For example, in chapter 1, we'll learn that setting clear expectations is a fundamental behavior all managers must do. We'll discuss why this behavior is important and why it might be hard to do. Often, we have subconscious biases or irrational tendencies that make it challenging for us to act in the most effective way possible. And often management behaviors feel counterintuitive to what we *think* is the right behavior. For example, more money may demotivate your team members instead of motivating them, a behavior that, on the surface, feels really wacky. Lastly—and here's the important part—we'll talk about how you can immediately start incorporating each management behavior into your day-to-day work.

Here's the crux: Managing is a muscle that needs to be built up, trained, and flexed. Therefore, there are small actions you can immediately start taking to practice the management behavior, as well as templates that help you train that behavior until it becomes muscle memory. If you were an engineer, no one would expect you to memorize all of the product specifications on your first day of work. Similarly, it's impossible to memorize the right script for a performance improvement conversation on day one of being a manager, yet we are expected to have those conversations anyway. That's why there are sample guides and other tools throughout the book and in the appendix to help you try out these new skills immediately and keep working on them. What's scary about managing is also what makes it rewarding: When you put these new behaviors into practice, you'll immediately see results. For example, your team members may become more motivated, or your team may let you know that a communication you shared fell totally flat.

Basketball star (and former Georgetown Hoya) Allen Iverson once said, "We talking about practice, man." But in management, your practice is also your game. So let's lace up the sneaks, get on the court, and start playing.

PART I
MANAGING AN INDIVIDUAL

PERFORMANCE

I remember the first hard conversation about performance I had when I became a new manager. One of my team members, Michael, was struggling to keep up with the pace of our work and with the rest of the team, and it fell on me to communicate that to him. I practiced the conversation in my head a whole bunch, and when I finally talked to Michael, I stumbled, I blabbed, and I quickly proved that my all-natural deodorant could not withstand a stress-inducing situation. I did a terrible job of telling Michael that he wasn't performing up to standard and that he may not have been right for his role.

In hindsight, I realized that as a new manager, I hadn't set clear expectations for him, given him constructive feedback, or supported his development. By the time I sat down with him to talk about his performance, there weren't very many options left. I ultimately had to let Michael go, and no doubt about it, my poor management of his performance was a main cause of his failure. Don't worry: Michael's story ends well. After he left our little consulting firm, he went to Harvard Law School and became a clerk for a Supreme Court judge (yes, *the* Supreme Court). The firm, on the other hand, went bankrupt. Clearly, Michael came out on top.

One of your most important responsibilities as a manager is managing your team members' performance. It's hard to manage people who aren't performing well. You'll spend countless hours giving feedback, coaching them to improve, and repeatedly clarifying your expectations of their work. But it might be even *harder* to manage a team member who is blowing it out of the water. You'll spend countless hours with the overper-formers to ensure that they have plenty of autonomy and lots of respon-sibility. You'll struggle to assign work that challenges them and reflects development goals they are inspired to work toward. Though few manag-ers will admit it, every so often, you'll wish for a team filled with solid B players. Mediocrity will let you breathe as a manager! Performance—both good and bad—will eat up a ton of your time, no two ways about it.

For the first part of our management journey, we are going to tackle performance. I'll answer questions like: How can you make sure your team members are set up for performance success? How can you help turn the boat around when your team members hit rocky performance waters? How can you help your team members build the skills and capabilities necessary for great performance? And how can you make sure your per-sonal grooming products are appropriate for hard performance conversa-tions? (Well . . . maybe not that one.)

CHAPTER 1

GREAT EXPECTATIONS

One summer, on a muggy Sunday afternoon, my dear friend Sarah and I were out for a vigorous power walk. Typical of such walks, as we were pumping our arms and swinging our hips, we were also discussing life and love, and she shared this gem of a quote that her father coined: "An expectation unarticulated is a disappointment guaranteed."[1]

An expectation unarticulated is a disappointment guaranteed.

This nugget of wisdom came up in the context of our dating lives, but, wow, it's a powerful concept for management. One thing you may notice as you start to manage is how often you will open an email, get off a Zoom call, or sit in a presentation, and experience a pervasive sense of disappointment.

The internal dialogue in your mind might go something like this:

You spent a week working and this *is what you have to show for it?*
Or
Yikes—this is what you think client-ready looks like?

Or

How could you possibly think this is good?

Or

Not only did you miss the boat on this one, but you weren't even in the harbor. Scratch that. You weren't even in a coastal state. The boat was in South Carolina, and you were in Kansas.

One of the dirty little secrets of managing is that it is a profoundly frustrating and disappointing job. Your team members will often swing and totally whiff with regards to your expectations. You end up redoing their work, saying harsh things about their abilities, or writing them off as less competent than you thought. This effect is particularly frustrating in a start-up environment, where work moves quickly and everyone just needs to *Get. Stuff. Done.*

But the other dirty little secret of managing is that much of the disappointment is our own fault as managers. We are disappointed because we haven't set and communicated clear, well-defined expectations for our people. Instead, our expectations go unarticulated.

Let me provide a little example to hammer home the point. Recently, a senior manager, Diane, came to me complaining about how a member of her sales team, Lalit, stunk at his job. Lalit didn't follow up on sales leads that Diane talked about during meetings; Lalit came to check-in discussions with Diane with nothing to talk about; and Lalit never brought ideas to the group about how to expand their client footprint. In sum, Lalit wasn't proactive, and Diane was super frustrated by him.

I'm sure you're patting yourself on the back right now, thinking, *I know the answer. I know why Diane failed as a manager. She never told Lalit to be proactive!* Well, my friends, you're wrong. Diane *did* tell Lalit multiple times that he should be more proactive. But she *didn't* show him what it looks like to her when a team member is proactive. She didn't clearly articulate her expectations for his behavior. Lalit was trying to be proactive but had no idea what Diane expected.

Expectation setting is one of the most important things you can do to be a great manager. It's a simple concept, but many managers—especially first-time managers—don't explicitly say what they want and need from their people. And when your team members are very junior (or it's their first job), not setting clear expectations becomes even more detrimental to everyone's success.

Don't try to manage by mind reading: to be a great boss, you have to set clear, well-defined, and explicit expectations for your team members.

To be a great boss, you have to set clear, well-defined, and explicit expectations for your team members.

Before I get into the *how* of good expectation setting, I want to talk a little bit about *why* it's hard to set expectations as a manager.

FEAR OF BEING A MICROMANAGER

You're hip, you're cool, you want everyone to like you, so you give your team freedom and flexibility. One of the reasons people love working for start-ups is that they don't really have a "boss" per se—just a friendly, slightly older person who sometimes checks in on their work. You're that person! In fact, you read once in a book—a book just like this one—that being hands-off is the best way to manage. You never want to be called a (gasp!) micromanager. You know how important it is to let people "figure things out" as opposed to telling them what to do. Your biggest fear is that your underlings will whisper about how you're an uptight micromanager who controls their lives.

But guess what? You're giving your people significant anxiety because they have no idea what to do. Micromanaging and setting clear expectations are very different beasts. In a totally unscientific study I conducted of ten junior people, I found that ten of them craved clearer direction from their manager and zero people wished their manager were vaguer and more wishy-washy about what she wanted.

It's true that working for a micromanager really stinks. They creepily hover over your laptop and, at times, grab your mouse to make direct changes to your work. My least favorite micromanager used to email me constantly throughout the day asking if my assignment was done. I wanted to say, "Dude, I'm spending so much time updating you on my progress that I have no time to actually get any work done."

A great manager sets clear expectations for what the team is looking to achieve and then lets her team member figure out the steps to get there; a micromanager insists on walking up every step with you while holding your hand and telling you where to place your foot and cautioning you that the step might be wet and insisting that you wear galoshes in case it gets wetter and then just decides that you shouldn't walk up the steps at all and she'll just do it for you.

So, no, micromanaging isn't the goal. Painting a clear picture of what "good" looks like is. Get over your fear of being a micromanager and be clear with what you want from your people.

> Micromanaging isn't the goal. Painting a clear
> picture of what "good" looks like is.

THE DUNNING-KRUGER EFFECT

The second reason why we struggle to set clear expectations is not our fault. It's a subconscious psychological bias called the Dunning-Kruger effect. (Note: this is also a great excuse in a relationship. When your partner yells at you for expecting them to be a mind reader, say, "It's not my fault. I'm experiencing a subconscious psychological bias!") This effect is named for the psychologists David Dunning and Justin Kruger, who found that newbies are overly confident in their ability to complete a task and will underestimate the time it takes to do it.[2] It also states that an expert will assume that a task that is easy for her to perform is also easy for others to complete.

So when you assign a junior employee a task that you think is easy, quick to do, and doesn't need explicit instructions, your biases may be getting in the way. You need to remind yourself that the tasks you've done hundreds of times may not be self-explanatory for your people. And you must also recognize that your people may erroneously think that they don't need more time or a deeper explanation to complete the task because of their own subconscious biases about their ability to do the task at hand.

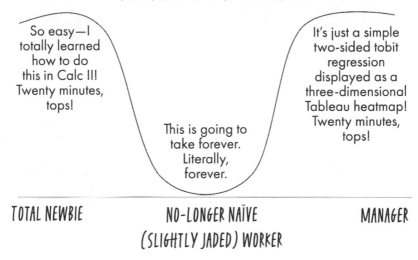

THE DUNNING-KRUGER EFFECT RUNNING RAMPANT IN THE WORKPLACE

So easy—I totally learned how to do this in Calc II! Twenty minutes, tops!

This is going to take forever. Literally, forever.

It's just a simple two-sided tobit regression displayed as a three-dimensional Tableau heatmap! Twenty minutes, tops!

TOTAL NEWBIE

NO-LONGER NAÏVE (SLIGHTLY JADED) WORKER

MANAGER

You consciously avoid setting expectations because you don't want to micromanage, and you subconsciously don't set expectations because you think your employees already know exactly what to do and how to do it.

———

Before I keep rambling on about where else cognitive biases wreak havoc in our lives, let's talk about the how: How do you set clear expectations for your team members?

You set clear expectations by always answering the following four questions:

1. What's the objective or end goal?

2. What does good look like?

3. What's the timing?

4. What are examples (if possible)?

THE SUPER-SIMPLE, FOUR-PRONGED APPROACH TO SETTING CRYSTAL CLEAR EXPECTATIONS		
FOUR PRONGS	**MORE INFO PLEASE**	**EXAMPLE**
1. What's the objective or end goal?	Why do you need or want this? What are we trying to achieve with this work? What impact will it have on the team, project, client, or customer?	"I'd like a weekly work plan that helps me see the status of each component of your work in one place. It helps me to quickly see where we are behind or on schedule without having to constantly email you for an update. It also allows us to see how delays may impact other pieces of work."
2. What does good look like?	What defines success for this activity or deliverable? How specific can you be about what a quality product looks like?	"A good work plan clearly shows detailed activities, who is doing what, and the expected timing for each of those activities. Additionally, it highlights where we are behind schedule or might run into issues. My strong preference is for this to be in a GANTT chart."
3. What's the timing?	When do you need the output by? When do you want to see a first draft? In what state (e.g., client-ready, draft form)?	"Moving forward, I'd like to see the work plan updated every week and for you to send it to me twenty-four hours before our weekly check-ins. Please send me your draft work plan tomorrow so that I know you're going in the right direction."
4. What are examples, if possible?	Share other work product, information, or content to support employee.	Share some work plans that you've used in the past.

When you give your team member an assignment, explicitly answer all of these questions. In fact, I would suggest writing down the answers to these questions, as it forces you to truly articulate what you expect. If you can't answer these questions, it might indicate that either the task isn't necessary or that you have no idea what you want out of this work.

These questions are a helpful framework to guide how you give instructions, but they aren't foolproof. Where do I see this approach falling down? No one would dispute the value of setting clear timelines, yet managers often don't want to tell people when an assignment is due or when they need a first draft. This comes back to the fear of micromanaging: For many of us, it's uncomfortable telling people exactly when we want something. We ask them when they think they can have it done, and we may not assert when we actually need it. The long-term result can be that you foster a team culture that is indifferent about deadlines. So be explicit about timing. You'll thank me later.

To sum up, dear reader, as a first-time manager, set clear expectations for your people. And when you think your expectations are clear enough, go back and make them even clearer. Push against the fear of having people think you're bossy or a micromanager. Your employees want to know what you expect and want to know what good looks like in your mind. And if you aren't clear about what you expect, expect to be disappointed.

> Set clear expectations for your people. And when
> you think your expectations are clear enough,
> go back and make them even clearer.

TL;DR

- Often, we don't articulate what we expect from our team members; this leads to disappointment, frustration, and feeling like our team members are incompetent.

- We don't set expectations because we're afraid of people thinking we're micromanagers; and we overestimate the abilities and competence of junior people.

- The solution is simple: Each time we assign a task or action, we should articulate why the task is necessary and its overall objective, define what good looks like, and state when we want the work done. If possible, we should provide examples of similar work.

- Continue to provide feedback when expectations aren't met and encourage our employees to speak up if they have questions about the expectations of an assignment.

CHAPTER 2

FEEDBACK IS LIKE UNDERWEAR: IT'S A GIFT YOU NEED, MAYBE NOT ONE YOU WANT

You've mastered the first—and potentially most fundamental—principle of being a great manager: setting clear expectations. Yet even with the absolute clearest and best-articulated expectations, your team members will still sometimes mess up, whiff the ball, miss the boat, and shoot a total brick. On the other hand, sometimes, your team members will hit it out of the park and cause you to beam with the pride of an overprotective, yuppie mother watching her firstborn receive a yellow participation ribbon during the kindergarten Olympics.

Either scenario warrants the next most important principle of being a great manager: giving well-structured feedback. If you're silently groaning right now, you're not alone. We hear all the time that feedback is important, that we *should* do it, and that our organizations value it. But in reality, we avoid giving feedback, and we avoid receiving it. When feedback does occur, it's poorly handled, confusing, and makes us feel as awkward as we felt at our first boy-girl dance in seventh grade. In this chapter, I'm going to convince you why feedback is so important, why it's so hard to give and receive, and most importantly, how to be a great giver and receiver of well-structured, effective feedback.

Let's start with a feedback story.

My first job out of college was at a management consulting firm. Clearly, I was well prepared for it since my work experience, at the time, amounted to a junior-year internship at a bank. I excelled at this internship given that my primary responsibilities were delivering holiday presents to clients around downtown Washington, DC, finding good lunch options with my fellow intern friend, Natalie, and selecting a "work outfit" from my college wardrobe. Sensing sarcasm? Yes. I actually had zero relevant experience for life at a consulting firm. Much to my chagrin, my first manager at this firm was a guy named Josh Hardy, who the other first-year consultants called "No Party Josh Hardy." That's because he took everything so seriously, despite being a mere one year older than us. All of my consultant friends were buddy-buddy with their managers, but Josh was like an unsuccessful mullet: business in the front . . . and business in the back.

Josh constantly told me what I was doing wrong, even things that I thought were trivial (or, dare I say, petty). For example, did Josh really have to harp on the fact that I used different color schemes in a PowerPoint deck or that my boxes on a slide weren't perfectly left aligned? Or what was the big deal when I showed up ten minutes late to an internal meeting? I had been a rower in college—showing up ten minutes late to morning classes was *early* in my book. Or the one that really got my goat: Did it really matter if and how I took notes during meetings? Hadn't I evolved past note taking when I graduated from school? Why did Josh constantly make me fix my meeting notes?

Yet, over the years, I have come to appreciate and be truly grateful for Josh Hardy. When I started my first job, I was a terrible consultant. I had no idea what I was doing and did some pretty bonehead things. But along with many other things, Josh took my development seriously and was a constant and effective giver of constructive feedback, despite my aversion to receiving that feedback. Josh made little tweaks in real time to how I did my work, how I helped or hindered the team, and how I interacted with our clients. I know that Josh's little tweaks changed my long-term career trajectory—little tweaks early on in someone's career have a huge impact later on.

Little tweaks early on in someone's career have a huge impact later on.

A graph best illustrates this:

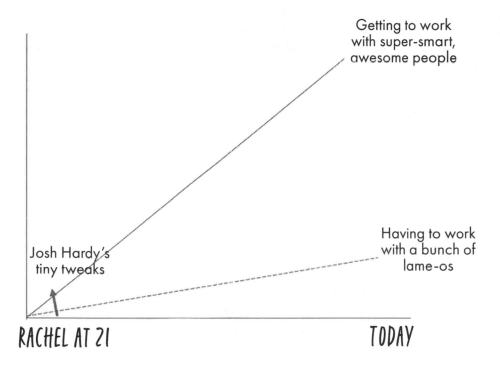

Getting to work with super-smart, awesome people

Having to work with a bunch of lame-os

Josh Hardy's tiny tweaks

RACHEL AT 21   TODAY

It's *much* harder to change someone's behavior after they've been doing it for years and years and years.

So, dear reader, to be a great manager, you must give constructive, well-structured, and frequent feedback. The power and responsibility you have in setting your team members on the right trajectory early on in their career is huge: Without feedback, your team members will not change those behaviors that, over time, may impede their professional and personal development. Without feedback, my twenty-one-year-old self's knuckleheaded habits would have been allowed to flourish.

To be a great manager, you must give constructive, well-structured, and frequent feedback.

But, you say, it's super awkward to give constructive feedback, especially when the person you're giving feedback to might be your age (or, even more awkwardly, older than you). You're probably not even 100 percent comfortable in your own job yet. You know you have tons of areas to improve upon, and you likely have a manager who might not be giving you the feedback *you* need to develop. What right do you have in telling someone else that what they're doing is wrong?

And to make matters worse, you want to be liked. You want to be accepted by others and not thrown out of your tribe. It's human instinct and rightfully so. With liking comes trust, closer collaboration, better communication, and a whole bunch of other wonderful benefits. You fear that if you give feedback, especially feedback that you *think* might hurt someone's feelings, your team members won't like you. You will be the mean manager.

Let me share a quick story about the so-called mean manager. Justine was the VP of operations at a start-up. She had a team member, Vit, who was falling short in a few areas of his work. Though his shortcomings frustrated Justine, she didn't give Vit feedback about them because he was new, and she didn't want to upset him and make him think she was a mean boss. She wanted to be liked. Well, fast-forward three months: the start-up's CEO saw that Vit was not improving and could not get the job done as needed. The CEO talked to Justine, and they decided that Vit's performance wasn't up to standard and that he would have to leave the company because of his poor performance. When Justine sat Vit down to share the news, Vit was totally shocked. He thought he was doing a great job. If he hadn't been performing well, why hadn't Justine told him sooner? How could Justine not have given him any feedback for three months?

Who's the mean manager now?

Not only do you have the right to tell someone when they aren't meeting the mark, but also you have the *obligation* to give feedback to those you manage. Helping your team members build the muscle of feedback and helping to reduce defensiveness in receiving constructive remarks is critical to building an anti-oppressive culture on your team. We often are so worried about stepping on toes, protecting feelings, and experiencing a little discomfort that we end up promoting a culture that is not focused on growth, progress, and inclusiveness. We inadvertently hold back our team members when we don't give feedback. And guess what? The feedback you give is going to be awkward, and it's going to be uncomfortable, and that's life. You still have to do it.

> The feedback you give is going to be
> awkward, and it's going to be uncomfortable,
> and that's life. You still have to do it.

Now you know the importance of feedback, and you're ready to override your fear of hurting your team's feelings or not being liked. The next question is, how do you give great feedback?

Great feedback is feedback that is clear, structured, data-driven, and changes or reinforces a behavior. Great feedback is kind and empathetic, as it comes from a desire to help the recipient improve and develop. Great feedback is timely and to the point. Great feedback can be constructive or positive.

THE SUPER-SIMPLE, REALLY OBVIOUS FEEDBACK PROCESS

Well-structured feedback follows a simple process.[1] Take a look at the next page to see how it works.

You might wonder what makes this process so powerful.

First, you're starting from a place of data ("I observed that you joined the meeting ten minutes late") as opposed to a place of judgment ("It's bad

| Explain the situation | Explain how it affected the client, project, or you | Pause for clarification | Suggest change in behavior |

ACTION / START THE SENTENCE WITH...

- "I observed..."
- "I noticed..."

- "The impact it had on me..."
- "The impact it had on our client..."
- "It made me feel..."

- Listen and answer any questions

- "Going forward you may want to consider doing the following differently..."

DESCRIPTION

- Explain the situation with as much detials possible
- Clarify the date/ time, and people involved
- Highlight the actions of the person receiving feedback

- Tell the person about your feelings resulting from their action
- Tell the person how it may have been perceived by the client or team

- Give the person receiving feedback a chance to ask clarifying questions and provide additional information
- You can also ask the recipient if this feedback resonates or what their reaction is

- Offer a constructive suggestion about ways the person could change/ improve their behavior
- Suggest timing of when you will check back in for observed behavior change

EXAMPLE

- "Troy, I noticed that the data you submitted for our therapy project was late."
- "The workplan specified that the data was due on Tuesday."

- "The late submission impacted the rest of the team, as we couldn't move forward with our analysis. The team waited all evening for the data."

- *Pause*
- *Listen*
- *Listen more*

- "Moving forward, communicate as early as possible if you need more time so we can figure out if you need additional support."
- "Is there anything else I can do to help you with meeting these deadlines?"

when you join meetings late"). Starting with data immediately brings the emotion down in a feedback conversation and helps the receiver of feedback be less defensive and more receptive to what you're about to say. It also leaves room for an alternative explanation. The feedback recipient might have been called into an emergency tête-à-tête with the chairperson of the board, which caused them to show up ten minutes late to your meeting.

Second, you're illustrating how the behavior impacts you, the team, or the client, thus helping the individual understand *why* this feedback is important. Going back to the example of my twenty-one-year-old self, Josh Hardy explained that different color schemes in my PowerPoint decks were not ideal because a client could interpret the different colors as a lack of attention to detail—which might make the client call into question our attention to detail in our financial models. Wow. That is far more powerful than just being told to change colors in a deck.

The last thing that makes this process so powerful is you're suggesting a change in behavior. Before you give any feedback, think about what this person could do differently to alter their behavior. If you can't think of anything, should you be giving the feedback? This last step creates accountability and ensures that the feedback you're giving is not "personal" (i.e., is not so closely connected to a person's identity that they can't change their behavior).

Let me further illustrate this last point. As we discussed, some people feel awkward giving feedback, but there are others who are almost *eager* to criticize. They get on their high horses when giving feedback and believe that they have license to discuss absolutely everything and anything. You know this person—the friend or coworker who rips into who you are as a person in the spirit of "transparency and honesty." The person who gives you feedback about how you're terrible at such-and-such because they just *care about you so much*. Does talking to this person usually make you feel better or motivate you to change yourself in any way? I'd bet not.

Effective feedback requires a clear example of how the individual can change or continue the specific behavior you are commenting on. For example, let's say I tell a team member, Mark, that his Boston accent lacks the refinement we want on our client-facing team. I use a well-structured and data-driven approach and feel proud of myself for having a difficult conversation and giving honest feedback. Mark leaves the feedback conversation confused and hurt: His accent is a part of who he is as a person. He can't all of a sudden start articulating his *r*'s. The feedback I gave was not actionable.

> **Effective feedback requires a clear example of how the individual can change or continue the specific behavior you are commenting on.**

Now let's rewind. Instead of criticizing his accent, I could give Mark feedback that he could slow down when he speaks, in case others are not able to follow. I could give Mark the suggestion of practicing his presentations with a timer to quantitatively measure how quickly he is speaking. Or I could give the suggestion that Mark repeatedly pause during a presentation to ask the audience if they have any questions or need a point repeated. This last step—suggesting a change in behavior—shows that as a manager you care about your team member improving and developing.

What else should you remember when you embark on this feedback process?

- **Don't sandwich constructive feedback**—that is, layering constructive feedback between two slices of positive (often overly cloying) feedback. Get right to the cheese: State the one piece of feedback you want to share and stick to that.

- **Don't "over-caveat" the feedback.** Comments like "I know you've been really stressed out and you're doing great in so many other areas and you've had so much on your plate and it's really not that big of a deal and . . ." muddy the message and confuse the recipient. Say the feedback in a concise and precise way.

- **Provide the feedback as close to when the behavior happens as possible**. No one likes to hear feedback about a situation from three months ago. The individual receiving the feedback has now lost three months in which they could have been altering their behavior. And the feedback may no longer be as relevant.

- **Approach the feedback discussion as exactly that: a discussion**. Be curious about the recipient's perspective or where the recipient thinks you, their manager, could help them improve upon their behavior. Provide space to listen to the recipient.

- **The feedback process is for both constructive *and* positive feedback.** We often do a terrible job of giving well-structured positive feedback. When we structure positive feedback in this way (and share how the person's behavior impacted the situation), it is motivating and inspiring. Repeatedly saying, "Great work!" is not motivating.

- **Last tip: just do it.** When you start giving feedback, it won't be perfect. You'll forget steps of the process. You might inadvertently insult someone. It's going to be awkward as heck. But keep doing it. I promise—you'll get better and each feedback conversation will no longer feel equivalent to when you were *forced* to go to school the day following the seventh-grade dance when all the cool kids learned you had a crush on super popular Scooter Voit-Fitzgerald.

BUT WHAT ABOUT RECEIVING FEEDBACK AS A MANAGER?

You are now great at giving well-structured, effective feedback. Well, the feedback story doesn't end here. To be a great manager, not only do you have to be great at giving effective feedback, but you also have to be great at receiving effective feedback from your team. Yup—you have to make sure that your team is able to give *you* feedback. Given that you're reading this book, you likely consider yourself a highly evolved individual who has a commitment to development. You rate yourself way up there on the self-awareness scale and believe that you are more actualized than the average Joe. In fact, you constantly ask for feedback from your own boss and pride yourself on being open to receive anything that comes from her mouth.

> To be a great manager, not only do you have to be great at giving effective feedback, but also you have to be great at receiving effective feedback from your team.

But what's much harder, despite our commitment to growth, is receiving feedback from those we manage. And why do we cringe when we receive feedback? It's our subconscious again. Let's dig in to why we have a hard time receiving feedback.

WHY WE CRINGE WHEN WE RECEIVE FEEDBACK

OUR REPTILIAN RESPONSE

It's actually an evolutionary instinct to run away from negative feedback (even though it's meant to be helpful). Research by psychologists Nathan DeWall and Brad J. Bushman builds on the primal fight-or-flight response we have to physical threats and shows that we subconsciously protect ourselves against nonphysical threats as well.[2] Our brains automatically code constructive feedback as a threat to our social standing, acceptance in community, and identity. When we hear someone tell us that we didn't do a good job on a project or that our tardiness needs to be improved, we automatically code that as a threat to our social safety. Just like we don't want to be eaten by a lion, we don't want to risk being socially rejected. This is why we automatically get defensive when we hear feedback. It's not because we are defensive individuals or don't want constructive feedback. We are biologically hardwired to defend. Therefore, it's really hard for us to rewire our primal instinct to be open and receptive to feedback when it comes our way.

WHAT YOUR REPTILIAN BRAIN IS THINKING...

OVERCONFIDENCE BIAS

We also have a hard time receiving feedback because we are subconsciously biased in thinking that we are much better at doing things than we actually are. Put another way, our subjective confidence in our own

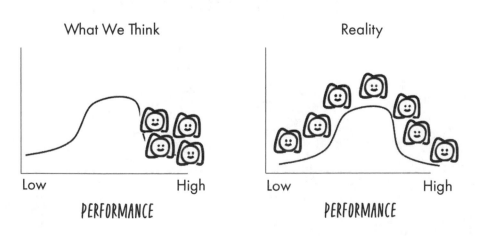

abilities is far greater than our actual objective abilities. This bias is perhaps best illustrated in the famous study by psychologist Ola Svenson, who showed that 93 percent of American drivers think they are better than the average driver.[3] So we are often shocked when we hear feedback that we are merely average at doing something—or even worse, that we are below average. Shocked and appalled!

ATTRIBUTION THEORY

We think our own shortcomings are the result of the environment around us, not something we have control over. Therefore, we subconsciously make excuses when we fall short of expectations. Social psychologist Bernard Weiner developed this powerful theory that explains so much about how we behave.[4] My friend who is late is lazy. When I am late, it's because the bus didn't come on time, the shower didn't get hot as quickly as usual, and my neighbor didn't stop blabbing when I was trying to leave the house. So when we are given constructive feedback, we immediately and unconsciously blame external factors for our shortcomings. We are not purposely trying to be defensive when we receive feedback: it's our subconscious again that is wreaking havoc.

ATTRIBUTION THEORY: HOW WE THINK ABOUT OUR OWN PERFORMANCE

When Things Go Right

I'm brilliant. I'm a hard worker. I'm really competent.

When Things Go Wrong

The directions weren't clear. I wasn't given enough time. Rob didn't do his part, which then hurt mine.

And when you are receiving feedback from people you manage, you might feel insecure about your new management abilities and shy away from asking your teammates about an area in which you know you may be deficient.

Lastly, it's really hard for individuals to speak up or dissent to authority figures, so your team may not offer constructive feedback willingly.

Case in point, I once asked my brother, John, about receiving feedback from the team he managed. He stated with no irony or self-consciousness: "I'm a great manager. I've never received feedback from my team."

When we do receive feedback from our team, the conversation goes something like this:

MANAGER: What feedback do you have for me as a manager?
TEAM MEMBER: Nothing, you're great!

OR

TEAM MEMBER: Well, everything is good, but if I had to think of something, I think you could provide me with more feedback.

OR

TEAM MEMBER: It would be great if you could be a little bit clearer with expectations. But no biggie because I know how busy you are, so it's probably my fault.

You then go on your merry way, incredibly proud of yourself for soliciting feedback from your team.

In later chapters, I am going to go in depth about how to train your team to speak up and speak out in situations where they might not feel comfortable. But for now, I want to highlight some tools you can use as a manager to ensure that you are receiving upward feedback from your team, and to ensure that you remain open to feedback when it comes your way—subconscious biases be darned.

1. **Ask for feedback**. Invite people to dance. Ask again. Keep asking. And then listen. When you receive the feedback, be open, welcome it, and be truly thankful to your team member for sharing. Take the feedback seriously and share with your team member how you are (or why you are not) changing the behavior they highlighted. Seek suggestions on specific, actionable ways you can improve and ask your team members to hold you accountable in your improvement.

2. **Separate receiving upward feedback from giving downward feedback**. Often, we jam our feedback ask at the end of a feedback conversation or performance review for our team member, which makes it even harder to receive honest, constructive comments. Heck, it's scary to critique your boss right before you get your bonus! Instead, schedule separate meetings for upward and

downward feedback. This distinction emphasizes that you care just as much about hearing their feedback as you do about providing your feedback to them.

3. **Make upward feedback part of your team's formal review process**. That is, let your team know that upward feedback is something you expect and that it is part of their role responsibilities. Praise (and reward) constructive and courageous upward feedback from your employees. Let your employee know if they're not meeting expectations with regards to giving you feedback.

4. **Lastly, send your team members an anonymous feedback survey**. It may take time for them to feel comfortable giving you constructive feedback, so help ease that burden a bit with a survey. Note: I also like to incorporate this survey into a manager's formal review (i.e., feedback from their team is part of all managers' formal performance assessments). Here are the questions I typically use:
   - This person as my manager provides me consistent and helpful feedback to aid in my development. (1 to 5 scale)
   - This person as my manager makes him/herself always available to me when I need him/her. (1 to 5 scale)
   - Given what I know of this person's management, I would always want him or her to be my manager. (1 to 5 scale)
   - What is one thing your manager could do to make your job easier?
   - Is there anything else you would like to add that would be helpful for your manager to develop?[5]

So, dear reader, to be a great manager, give well-structured, effective feedback. And to be an even greater manager, get your team to give *you* well-structured, effective feedback. Embrace your inner Josh Hardy and remember that it's not just your responsibility but your obligation to make sure your people develop and grow through timely, frequent feedback.

TL;DR

- Your job as a manager is to provide constructive, timely feedback. You will hurt your employee's long-term career prospects if you do not provide feedback.

- We are terrible at giving feedback because we want to be liked and we know that individuals have a hard time receiving feedback.

- We are terrible at receiving feedback because we are biologically hardwired to run away from threats to our ego; we also believe our performance is better than it typically is.

- Effective feedback starts from a place of data and objectivity and provides actionable modifications to behavior at the end of the feedback.

- Great managers also actively solicit feedback from their team members; praise and reward those team members who show courage in giving hard feedback.

- Just do it. If there is one thing you take away from this chapter, it's that you should just start giving feedback. It will be awkward at first, but the important thing is that you start doing it.

CHAPTER 3

OWN IT!
(YOUR DEVELOPMENT,
THAT IS)

’m not a particularly nostalgic person, but my next story also comes from my first job out of college. I learned many valuable life lessons as a young, fresh-faced employee, many of which I have only recently come to fully appreciate. These include wisdoms like, "Just because work is paying for dinner doesn't mean you need to order a fried macaroni-and-cheese-ball appetizer at every meal." And, "When you have nothing to talk about at a team gathering, frequent-flyer programs are always a safe and peppy topic." And, "When you want your intern to do your work, tell them that it's a great growth opportunity."

But probably the most important lesson I learned early in my career was the concept of "owning my own development." At my first job, there was a strong expectation that each employee was the primary owner of their own development. Our managers and mentors were there to support us in our growth, but we needed to actively drive the path we wanted to take in our careers. Each person had the responsibility to determine what they wanted to do, how they wanted to grow, and what skills they wanted to build.

I'm sure the following scene feels really familiar: Your team member asks for formal training. They ask for a well-defined path to promotion. They ask you for the list of capabilities you want them to develop in their role. They look to you to have all the answers about how exactly they should grow under your tutelage. But perhaps your organization is brand new and doesn't have any training programs in place. Or your organization doesn't have well-mapped career journeys in place. As a manager, your resources and time are limited. Often, you aren't able to also take on the responsibility of being the primary driver of each team member's development.

What you *can* do as a manager is help your team members reframe their approach to development. Specifically, you can push them to consider their own development as *their* key responsibility. Your team members will feel empowered to grow, develop, and build skills despite limited structure and resources from your organization. And they won't look to you for all of the answers. They'll look to you for guidance, mentoring, and support.

There are two reasons why this approach works.

First, as I will discuss far more extensively in chapter 7 of this book, research shows that when we set and are responsible for our own goals, we are more likely to achieve them.[1] Put another way, your team member who identifies their own development goals is going to be more motivated and excited about tackling those goals than a team member who is handed a set of goals from you.

Second, each individual member of your team has different career aspirations, different strengths and weaknesses, and different areas of interests. You cannot create a one-size-fits-all development plan for all individuals on your team. Granted, there are competencies that you expect every team member to have, but you can't expect every team member to follow an identical growth path. Therefore, you need an approach that allows for unique development goals that are aligned with a team member's career interests as well as to the needs of the role and organization.

> You cannot create a one-size-fits-all development
> plan for all individuals on your team.

How do you help your team members own their own development? The primary tool I use is the individual development plan,[2] which asks your team members to think through a set of development questions. It helps them to articulate what skills and capabilities they want to develop in the short term as well as where they want their career to be in the long term. The development plan shows how each employee wants to grow, allowing you, as the manager, to support each employee in the way that makes sense for them. It also helps to highlight early on the employee's expectations and aspirations.

For example, your employee, Duane, writes in his plan that his one-year goal is to be promoted to a manager. You think that Duane needs more than a year to gain the skills required for a promotion. The development plan allows you to start having conversations early in the year with Duane about the likelihood of promotion or what skills are required to get to the next level. This helps to prevent Duane from being sorely disappointed when promotion time comes around, and prevents you from being shocked that Duane actually thought he was ready for promotion! (Remember overconfidence bias? You'll repeatedly be floored by team members who think they are ready for promotions.)

What's powerful about the individual development plan is that it pushes the individual to structure their development at the *capability* level. It helps the team member to break down their goals into the capabilities that are required to achieve a higher-order goal.

Let's step through an example. Your team member, Mia, wants to gain more client management skills. She describes that the way to achieve this is by doing more client-facing work. Mia might then be disappointed if there isn't more client-facing work to take on or if the client-facing work that is available is too high stakes for her. Mia might feel defeated in her ability to develop in her role.

But a capability approach to development pushes Mia to think about what capabilities are required to be a great client manager. These capabilities might include presentation and public-speaking skills (in order to effectively pitch clients and speak in front of a high-stakes audience); negotiation and difficult conversation skills (in order to effectively push back on clients in a thoughtful and effective way without harming the relationship); and active listening skills (in order to easily and seamlessly pivot between topics that might be on your client's mind). These are all capabilities Mia can work on *without having to work directly with a client.*

INDIVIDUAL DEVELOPMENT PLAN TEMPLATE

1. ONE-YEAR GOALS
What are your career goals over the next year at X in general? What role do you hope to play at X by the end of the year? How do you hope to be viewed by your fellow employees?

2. THREE-YEAR (LONGER-TERM) GOALS
What are your long-term career goals? Where do you see yourself in three years? What title or role do you hope to achieve within X? What do you hope to achieve outside of X?

3. CAPABILITIES/SKILLS

What are the three capabilities or skills you want to build over this year?	What are the activities, projects, or training you will do to build this skill or capability you identified? Be as specific as possible.	How will you measure success? What tangible outcome or metric will measure your improvement?	Who will support you in building this capability?
•			
•			
•			

Another great aspect of the individual development plan is that it pushes the team member to articulate the activities they will do to build these capabilities. For example, a team member, Jai, wants to build deeper analytical skills in his role. He lists a set of activities that could help him achieve this: signing up for a statistics course on Coursera, shadowing a data scientist on the team, and working on a side project that involves heavy data analysis. Jai can also identify individuals inside or outside of your organization that can support him in achieving those skills.

Development plans are dynamic. Your team members should frequently revisit the plans and update the plans as they build new skills or identify new activities to undertake. As a manager, your role is to support them in filling out the plan, provide guidance in what capabilities they might want to focus on developing, and help identify the activities that they can undertake to achieve their goals. I also recommend that team members share their development plans widely: They might realize that their peers have similar development goals and, as such, can get ideas about potential activities to undertake and can help hold each other accountable in working on their plans. And the most important thing for your team members to remember about their development plans is that *they own them.*

TL;DR

- To be a great manager, empower your team members to own their own development. This means that the team member is responsible for identifying areas of development and being proactive in how they think about their long-term career growth.

- The concept of having ownership of one's own growth is important for two reasons: When we set our own goals, we are more likely to be committed to them and to achieve them; it's hard to have a one-size-fits-all approach to employee growth and development.

- An individual development plan is a tool you can use with all of your employees to help them identify the areas in which they want to develop and grow.

- The power of the individual development plan is that it forces your team members to identify specific capabilities they can develop, as opposed to just high-level goals that might be dependent on outside factors in order to achieve them.

CHAPTER 4

THE COACHING PLAYBOOK

A few years ago, I attended an intensive yoga and meditation retreat. I was struggling with aspects of my life and couldn't seem to get out of my own way. Much of the retreat was spent in a group-therapy setup. After hours of intense yoga, we discussed our fears, what holds us back in life, and what our ideal state of being in this world is. Often, a retreat participant would stand up to share a situation they were struggling with in front of the group, and the retreat guru/yogi-to-the-stars would, without fail, ask the following questions:

- What do you fear about this situation?

- What is preventing you from taking action?

- What's at risk if you don't take action in this situation?

- What's your ideal outcome in this situation?

The results in answering these questions were powerful: The struggling yogi gained clarity and a new perspective on how to face their challenging situation and, importantly, devised their own path on how to move forward. Guided by the guru, the individual came to their own conclusions about what was holding them back.

After the haze of the week subsided and I returned to civilian life, I realized that the approach we were using at the yoga retreat was almost identical to the approach a great manager takes to coach their team members.

As we become managers, we hear a lot about "coaching." We are told that we should be *player-coaches*; we are told that we should coach our teams; and we might even be lucky enough to get our own executive coaches. We hear colleagues and friends talk about how their coaches have transformed their lives, how their coaches helped them step into their leadership power, or how their coaches gave them the confidence to change careers.

But what is coaching? And how do you develop the skills to be a great coach for your team members? Coaching is a technique used to help guide someone toward greater self-awareness, clarity on decisions and choices, and reflection on past behaviors. In practice, coaching looks like a set of thoughtful and thought-provoking questions and prompts, with the coach helping the coachee explore different outcomes. Unlike a mentoring or feedback conversation, a coaching conversation doesn't involve the coach immediately telling the coachee what to do differently or what the coach would do in the same boat. The coach helps the coachee build the decision-making muscle.

As a manager, you use coaching along with feedback and other more formal performance conversations to help your team member develop. For example, you might provide real-time feedback after a client presentation. You might provide coaching to your employee to help them determine how to respond to a difficult client request. Both techniques are necessary for the growth of your team member, but are different in their approach and outcomes.

Coaching is a powerful tool to have in your toolbox as a manager. And all managers—regardless of level of seniority—can build their coaching capabilities. Before we explore how to do that, let's go over why coaching is such an important component of helping your employees strengthen their performance and ultimately develop and grow.

MENTORING VS. FEEDBACK VS. COACHING
as applied to a pain-in-the-neck client situation

MENTORING

What's worked for me in my career is to approach conflict head on with the client.

I would try to solve this by running at the disagreement head on.

FEEDBACK

I observed that you were silent when the client asked for work outside our scope.

You should push back harder on the client and not be afraid of conflict.

COACHING

What seems to be the main obstacle you're facing with the client?

What's your ideal outcome with your client?

What are the potential options?

WHY COACHING HELPS YOUR TEAM MEMBERS "GET JACKED"

1. **It builds the muscle of proactivity.** As we discussed in chapter 1, proactivity is a critical skill you will want (and need) your team members to develop. The best team members are the ones who anticipate your needs, seek out solutions instead of problems, and actively provide suggestions of what to do as opposed to always looking to you (their manager) for the answers. Proactive employees develop their own opinions about what course of action to take and feel empowered to speak up. But proactivity is a capability that needs to be built. Coaching helps to build that capability in your team members by training them to evaluate decisions, be reflective, and develop their own opinions about things. It helps them to have conviction.

2. **It builds the muscle of ownership.** In coaching, you rarely tell the coachee what they *should* do. You might help the coachee outline their next steps in a situation and keep them accountable in following through on those steps. But in coaching, you guide the coachee to chart their own path forward as opposed to dictating that path for them. This empowers your team member to develop their own course of action to address a challenge. When an individual has input or is the primary decision maker, they are far more likely to take ownership over that decision and be committed to executing the plan. At first, this might be scary for an employee: They may be nervous that their decision is wrong and that the responsibility of that decision falls on them. But over time, coaching builds the muscle of ownership and helps the employee feel comfortable with committing to and owning a decision.

3. **It builds the muscle of trust.** As a coach, you ask a set of questions to test assumptions and biases, and discover alternative paths. You help your coachee uncover hidden narratives and help them move past mental barriers. Asking thoughtful, coaching questions with the person you are managing—and actively listening to their answers—adds a new, deeper dimension to the boss-employee relationship. Through coaching, you are actively building trust with your team members by giving them the opportunity to be open in a safe and vulnerable way. And trust is critical to the manager relationship: Research has long shown that trust increases communication, improves collaboration, and reduces negative types of conflict, among many other wonderful things.[1] Many people ask: How can I build trust with my team? Coaching is a great way to do so.

Okay, so *how* can you start coaching your team members? First, I want to acknowledge that there are training programs, certifications, and schools built around becoming a qualified coach. And if you've ever had the opportunity to be coached by someone who is truly phenomenal, you realize that great coaching is simultaneously an art form, a scientific discipline, and an innate gift. But coaching itself is a basic tool that you can start implementing immediately without all of the training and courses.

> **Great coaching is simultaneously an art form, a scientific discipline, and an innate gift. But coaching itself is a basic tool that you can start implementing immediately.**

How do you do it? Start asking thoughtful questions. Next time you are about to suggest a solution or be directive to your team member, instead ask a clarifying or probing question first that allows them to reflect or consider other options. You could ask one or two questions to push your team member to go deeper into their thinking, or you could ask a whole series of questions. The more you ask coaching questions, the better you'll get at actively listening for answers and asking relevant follow-up questions.

Here are some other tips to becoming a great coach:

- **Ask open questions** that require more than a yes or no response.

- **Ask questions one at a time.** Early on, you may have a tendency to pile on questions, especially as you look to get context and information.

- At the beginning of the conversation, **ask for context but push for the context to be brief**, and be comfortable asking for the context to be shorter. Often, we get so caught up in the story of a situation (he did this, I did that, then this happened) that we miss the nuggets of what actually matter (how I reacted, how it made me feel, what do I want to do next).

- **Approach the conversations with true curiosity** as opposed to fishing for an answer. Example: Why didn't you do this? (fishing) vs. What prompted you to choose that path? (curiosity)

- **Embrace the silence**, even when it's awkward. Let silence linger—don't try to fill the silence with comments; give your coachee the space to think and process.

- **Repeat back what you've heard** to show that you're listening and, more importantly, test that you're understanding the conversation accurately. Often when something is played back to us, it allows us to reflect on what we said from a different perspective.

- When possible, **set up next steps** from the conversation. A powerful outcome of a coaching conversation is often a clear set of action steps and an accountability mechanism (which could be as simple as a check-in email a few days later).

And my final coaching tip for you? When you first start coaching, focus on a few impactful and simple questions. Ask the following:

1. What concerns you about this situation?

2. What do you fear most about taking the action or having the discussion?

3. What is your ideal outcome?

4. What would be an alternative way to approach this that you haven't considered?

5. If you could do it over again, what would you do differently?

6. What would you need to be true for this to be a success?

In the appendix, I've listed a whole bunch more useful coaching questions.[2] When I first started coaching, I printed out a list of my favorite coaching questions and kept them on my desk. When I would get stuck in a conversation, I'd glance over to my list and see if any of the questions resonated. Over time, the questions became second nature.

One of the most rewarding things I've found as a manager is when I'm deep in a coaching conversation with an individual and the light bulb goes off: a solution, an idea, or an opening comes to the person. They discover something new about the situation that they hadn't seen a mere twenty minutes earlier. This experience, for me at least, is far more powerful than providing my team member helpful advice. There is something beautiful about witnessing and aiding an individual as they discover something on their own. Coaching allows for that.

TL;DR

- Coaching is a technique that allows a coachee to build the muscle around decision-making and to evaluate behaviors and options.

- You don't need to be a professional coach to deploy this technique with your team members—anyone can be a coach, and it's a great tool to help your employees develop.

- Part of why coaching is so powerful is because it empowers individuals to come to their own conclusions; it also helps individuals build the capability of being proactive and solution oriented. In essence, folks are more likely to do something when they make the decision themselves to do it.

- To start coaching, just start asking questions! Thoughtful questions coupled with active listening are all you need to start your journey to be a great coach.

CHAPTER 5

MANAGING PERFORMANCE ANXIETY

After reading the first four chapters of this book, you are an outstanding coach and the best expectation setter. You give your team members thoughtful, frequent feedback, and your team is clear on how to develop and grow under your auspices. Yet, despite such management skill, you still might have an underperforming member on your team. They're struggling to improve, and you are starting to become concerned about whether they're going to be successful in the long run in your organization. Or you might have a team member who just can't seem to get to the next level—their peers are being promoted, but they can't make the leap. In both cases, a performance improvement plan (PIP) is in order. A PIP is a tool that helps your team member understand how they can improve and helps you provide a clear, structured set of actions for that improvement.

I'm not going to lie: Putting someone on a performance improvement plan, especially the first time you do it, may not be fun. There will likely be uncomfortable moments, perhaps some emotions, and a potential shark tank of defensiveness to swim around. But great managers know how powerful a tool a PIP can be. It provides clarity to a messy situation and helps both the manager and team member feel empowered. PIPs are much demeaned. But when used well, they are effective at ensuring that your team continues to thrive.

Let me start with a little story about a PIP and a protagonist I adore: my little brother, Thomas. By the time you read this book, Thomas will be well on his way to becoming a physician. But prior to Thomas's medical career, he was—for a very short period of time—a consultant. As his first job out of college, Thomas had been working at this consulting company for about a year when his manager and his manager's manager called him into a conference room for a discussion about his performance. As he sat down, they presented him with a performance improvement plan. Thomas was shocked and confused. As his bosses started going through the materials, Thomas began to assume that the performance improvement plan was just a sneaky formality that signaled an imminent firing. Before his manager and manager's manager had a chance to finish, Thomas thanked them for the opportunity to work at the company, stated that he didn't agree with the PIP, and resigned on the spot. Without waiting for a reaction, he walked out of the room and then out of the building.

I love this story, not only because it gives me an opportunity to embarrass my baby brother but also because of what it tells us about the pitfalls even the most seasoned managers make regarding performance. A manager should never surprise a team member with a performance improvement plan, nor should that manager bring up areas of feedback only once a year. On the other hand, a team member shouldn't feel the need to react so brashly and rashly to constructive feedback. Nor should a manager use a performance improvement plan as a check-the-box, dot-the-i's step to fire someone. And an employee shouldn't interpret an improvement plan as a sly way of pushing them out of the company. The list goes on and on.

As a manager, you will need to understand when someone is underperforming and what to do about it. To be a great manager, you should not be afraid to use performance improvement plans to clearly articulate how your team members can get better, as long as the performance improvement plans are coupled with ongoing feedback, a clear understanding by all of what they are (and what they aren't), and a true commitment by the manager to help the employee improve.

> To be a great manager, don't be afraid to use
> performance improvement plans to clearly
> articulate how team members can get better.

One reason why PIPs are so powerful is that they force the manager to specifically and concisely articulate why an employee is not meeting expectations. Often, managers do a lot of hand-waving about why someone is an underperformer: We talk in generalities, we attribute underperformance to personality traits, and we ding someone for not meeting our performance expectations that we never actually explicitly articulated. And we do this because it's hard to accurately assess someone else's performance.

WHY IT IS HARD TO OBJECTIVELY ASSESS PERFORMANCE

THE LADDER OF INFERENCE

The ladder of inference, a model created by Chris Argyris, one of the founding grandfathers of the field of organization development, describes how we quickly and subconsciously take data and make high-level inferences about individuals and their behaviors.[1] These inferences may not be valid and may not be representative of an individual's actual performance.

What we often do as managers is evaluate an individual's performance from a place of inference. We decide that someone is unprofessional because they missed a deadline. We quickly infer that someone is an underperformer because their last presentation failed to address client questions. But we never go back to the data to understand and explain why we came to that conclusion. The conclusion that an individual is unprofessional or an underperformer was made from a hasty inference, and that conclusion might be wrong.

The ladder of inference goes hand-in-hand with attribution theory, the concept we first discussed in chapter 2. When something goes wrong for someone else, we attribute it to shortcomings in someone's innate personality. A flawed presentation means our team member is not smart enough (though our own flawed presentation was due to not getting right information from others, our computer malfunctioning, or our dog distracting us).

THE LADDER OF INFERENCE

What Nico Is Thinking

We can't count on Jasper. He's unreliable.

Jasper always comes in late.

Jasper knew exactly what time the meeting was to start. He deliberately came in late.

The meeting was called at 9:00 a.m. and Jasper came in at 9:30 a.m. and didn't say why.

Pool of Data
The Meeting is at 9:00 a.m.

What Jasper Is Thinking

Nico is an unappreciative co-worker and I do not like working on his teams.

Nico always thinks his time is more valuable than anyone else's.

Nico is not acknowledging the trouble I went through to make his meeting.

I left my other 9:00 a.m. meeting early in order to attend Nico's meeting.

CONFIRMATION BIAS

Once you anchor on your team member's poor performance, you have a natural (and subconscious) tendency to seek out examples that confirm the theory that your team member is an underperformer and ignore the information that might disprove this theory. For example, you believe Kathy has poor attention to detail because the report she passed in had grammatical errors and a few typos. Next week, you notice that an email from Kathy had a misspelled word. And the following week, Kathy forgot to print enough copies of her presentation for the team brainstorming. Your theory has been confirmed. Kathy has poor attention to detail. What you ignore are the twelve reports she wrote this year that were impeccable with no errors. Or the thousands of emails she sent that were perfect. That's confirmation bias at play.[2]

A PIP helps to counteract the ladder of inference, attribution theory, and confirmation bias by forcing you to explicitly write down what areas a team member is underperforming and provide examples of those areas. An effective PIP will be a lot of work on your part as the manager. Be prepared that a PIP is often as much work for the manager as it is for the employee.[3] Now let's talk about *how* you put together a PIP.

STRUCTURING A PIP

A good PIP has the following components (see appendix for PIP template).

AREAS OF IMPROVEMENT

These are the three to four *most* important areas that the employee needs to improve in order to meet expectations or get to the next level in their career. Focus on the big ones—the areas that must be improved. Listing too many areas of development is confusing and hard to measure. Use examples where possible. For example, show where the team member fell short on attention to detail or where their analytical skills did not meet client expectations.

ACTION PLAN FOR IMPROVEMENT

Articulate three to five activities that the individual can start doing to demonstrate that they are showing improvement on the areas above. This section is the hardest part of the PIP to put together as it forces you to find ways for the employee to demonstrably show progress and ways for the employee to clearly practice these areas of improvement. If there are metrics you can use to objectively demonstrate improvement, add those in!

For example, you may ask for the employee to put together a weekly work plan that they will send to you every Monday morning that clearly lays out their priorities for the week. You may talk about a big project in this section and what improvement clearly looks like for that project. This section of the PIP gives your employee something to tackle and work on, and makes the PIP about action, not just a bunch of areas where your employee has fallen short.

CLEAR TIMELINE

Articulate when and how you will check in with your team member and what the process is for those check-ins. Communicate when decisions will be made and how long the PIP lasts. For example, the PIP might be two months long, with formal check-ins every two weeks.

Make sure you stick to the timeline as dictated in the PIP and commit to these check-ins. Continue to give feedback. If an employee is knocking it out of the park, take her off the PIP. If the employee comes to the end of the PIP and is making improvement, but not enough, you may want to extend the PIP a little longer and perhaps add some additional material. If the employee is not making any progress, you may then move forward with transitioning the employee out of your organization—but, most importantly, this will not be a surprise.

INITIATING A PIP

But, Rachel, you're thinking, *now I have to tell the employee they're going on a PIP. How do I do that so they don't storm out?*

Many managers are comfortable putting together a PIP and in theory are wholeheartedly onboard with the idea. Things often fall apart—especially for first-time managers—in having the initial PIP conversation. I get it. It's scary to tell a team member that they are underperforming and that their place at the organization is not guaranteed. In coaching new managers, I often spend the most time role-playing and practicing the PIP conversation before the manager actually has it. Here are some ways to effectively have that conversation.

NO SURPRISES

My suggestion is to give your employee a heads-up that you are going to have a conversation about performance. Something simple, like, "At our next one-on-one, I'd like to discuss areas where I see need for improvement and talk about how we can work on those areas together." Here's the inevitable rub: You send that email a day before the one-on-one, and your employee spends twenty-four hours being anxious about the conversation. You don't send the email, and the employee is totally shocked and taken off guard about what the conversation is about. Hopefully, you are giving feedback along the way so that your team member isn't surprised by the performance conversation. If they are surprised, take a hard look at if and how you have been communicating performance expectations along the way. Your team member should not be shocked by the PIP.

WHEN POSSIBLE, CO-CREATE THE PIP

When you enter the PIP conversation, you may want to print out a draft of the *Areas of Improvement* and *Plan Moving Forward* sections of the PIP and walk through those sections with your employee. But approach it as a conversation: Your employee might have other suggestions of how they can demonstrate success that might be helpful to add. If possible, have the employee help to jointly finalize the PIP. As a manager, you may outline the high-level areas that the employee needs to work on, then work with the employee to articulate ways that the employee is going to demonstrate competence and improvement.

COMMUNICATE YOUR PIP PHILOSOPHY

During the conversation, reinforce your approach to PIPs: These are meant to help get the employee over the performance hump and make sure that you, as their manager, are being clear about what needs to get done. Reinforce that PIPs are not a formality to being let go, but rather a tool for improvement and that you are committed to helping your team member improve. And make sure that you are communicating your PIP philosophy before your team members are ever put on one.

Here are some additional principles to include in your PIP philosophy:

Guiding Principles for PIPs

1. A PIP can be created any time throughout the year.

2. Err on the side of putting someone on a PIP earlier rather than later in a person's performance journey. This also means that people get taken off PIPs early when they demonstrate improvement.

3. PIPs are for team members who are not meeting expectations in their current roles as defined by their managers—this could mean a team member who is having difficulty making the leap to the next level and just can't seem to get promoted.

4. PIPs are consistent across the team in terms of structure and management of the process. Every PIP is given the same attention, care, and commitment.

5. PIPs are *not* a check-the-box step to let someone go; rather, they are used to provide precise, clear expectations for improvement on a defined timeline. We frequently celebrate team members who were on PIPs and got promoted.

6. Nothing in a PIP should ever be a surprise—at the very least, the manager should verbally talk through what is in the PIP before the written document is produced. In an ideal setting, the team member should be getting real-time feedback along the way.

A number of years ago, there was an associate in my organization, Marie, who was an incredibly hard worker but could not seem to advance in her career. Her peers were getting promoted while she was stagnant. Marie's manager, Zara, knew she was underperforming and frequently gave her the feedback that she was not quite cutting it. Marie, hearing that feedback, put in more hours to get better, which actually made her performance worse. Well, we finally asked Zara to put Marie on a formal PIP. This forced Zara to specifically and clearly articulate why Marie was falling short. It forced Zara to be precise with her feedback—even if that feedback was hard for Marie to hear. And through the process of putting together the PIP, we realized that Zara hadn't been giving Marie the truly tough feedback she needed to improve. What happened when Marie received the PIP? She was relieved and energized. Finally, it was crystal clear what she needed to do to improve. Marie dove into the PIP and was taken off the PIP before it ended. Late that year, she got promoted and became one of the top senior associates in her class.

Use PIPs. They will make your life easier. They will help you to clearly identify why someone is not improving and help them to improve. And they will ensure that you are properly documenting actions you have taken to help someone grow in your organization. I can't guarantee that an employee won't walk out of a PIP conversation and never look back, but the chances of that happening will be much slimmer if you take the time to thoughtfully and carefully put together a detailed performance improvement plan.

TL;DR

- It's important for you, as a manager, to be comfortable putting your team members on performance improvement plans when they are not meeting expectations of performance.

- When assessing someone's performance, there are subconscious biases that may inhibit us from being completely objective with how someone is performing; these include the ladder of inference, attribution theory, and confirmation bias.

- A good PIP has a defined timeline and is concise: it should focus on three to four areas of improvement and a short set of clear action items for the person to work toward.

- Along with a clear process, you can create a positive culture toward PIPs by celebrating when an individual comes off of a PIP and holding up positive examples of when a PIP was helpful.

A FINAL NOTE ON PERFORMANCE

Astute readers might note the absence of a chapter on end-of-year performance reviews. Over the years, I have given countless performance reviews and designed and implemented multiple performance review processes for start-ups. I have also designed multiple performance review processes that we didn't call performance reviews, didn't happen exactly on an annual basis, but essentially functioned exactly like a standard review process. Here's why there is no chapter on the standard performance review: There are lots of ways to design performance reviews, and a whole bunch of researchers and companies have put in a whole bunch of money trying to figure out what works and what doesn't work for formal performance reviews.[1] This has resulted in companies spending huge amounts of time and money rehauling their performance systems and then changing them back. This has also resulted in countless managers around the world spending hours filling out paperwork, checking boxes, and providing reviews that are at times useful but typically are not very useful for the amount of energy put into them. Managers hate doing reviews, and employees experience anxiety when they are impending, as they often have no idea what is going to be said in the review.

You should do performance reviews in some form or another: They are helpful to document progress and performance and are good forcing mechanisms for those managers who might otherwise be lazy when it comes to developing their teams.[2] But for great managers (that's you, my dear reader), it's more important to focus on frequent, real-time feedback that occurs throughout the year that helps your team to grow and develop. It's more important to focus on using tools like performance improvement plans as soon as you see a need to in order to address performance challenges as opposed to waiting for annual or biannual reviews And it's critical to be clear about what expectations you have of your team members so that when the reviews do come, there are no surprises about what you expected of your team and how they performed relative to those expectations. So rate your teams, fill the forms, have the formal conversations, but never let annual reviews be a stand-in for other, more important ways to manage performance on your team.

MOTIVATION

Know that feeling you get when you've been working on an activity and the time flies? You look up, and hours have passed without you realizing? You enter a state of flow, you're excited and inspired by the task at hand, your brain is engaged, you're learning, and you feel challenged. You forget to eat. You forget to shower. "Eye of the Tiger" is running on constant repeat in your brain. And when you finally complete what you've been working on, a huge sense of accomplishment washes over you. You sit back, proud of what you've done. Then, to top it all off, someone who is important in your life acknowledges your creation and tells others what you've accomplished.

I've just described the ultimate motivation scenario. Put simply, motivation is the drive and desire to do something. Motivation can be driven by internal reasons—such as a desire to learn or be challenged—or by external reasons—such as a desire to gain status or earn a financial bonus. Either way, motivation is critical for management. As managers, one of our primary responsibilities is motivating our teams to do their best work and be fulfilled when doing it.

There are many ways to motivate your team members (including beginning every team meeting with a song from *Jock Jams*[1]). And not every team member is going to be motivated in exactly the same way. In the prior chapters, I talked about performance—how to help your team members get better at what they are doing. In the next few chapters, I am going to talk about how to help your team members get jazzed up about what they are doing. Spoiler alert: There is no silver bullet to motivation. Sometimes, a desire to learn a new skill will be a huge motivator for a team member. They will go above and beyond the call of duty because they enjoy being challenged and learning along the way. Other times, cold hard cash will be the primary reason your team member gets out of bed. Different ways of motivating often have trade-offs and sometimes unintended consequences. For the next part of your management journey, we're going to explore how you can become the Tony Robbins (or insert preferred motivational speaker *here*) of managing your team. So without further ado, let's get motivating!

CHAPTER 6

THE TRIFECTA OF MOTIVATION: ACHIEVEMENT, POWER, AND AFFILIATION

When I'm interviewing job candidates, one of my favorite questions to ask is "What do you love about your current job? What gets you fired up about going in to work every day?"

I find it to be a great window into a person's psyche. I learn what drives this person and how this person derives meaning in their day-to-day work. And the answers run the gamut. Some folks love the people they work with and immediately start gushing about their teams. Others love the challenge of their role and go on about how they are constantly learning. Others talk about the responsibility they have to their organization's mission. One guy told me he loved how short his commute was (he was not joking, and, no, he didn't get the job).

Each of us is motivated by different things. For each of the people that you manage, could you answer the following?

- What does my team member love most about their role?

- Why would my team member leave their current job?

- What's the best way to reward or praise my team member?

As a manager, understanding what uniquely drives your employees is critical for understanding how to incentivize, develop, and structure work for your team for maximum motivation. Before I discuss the specific levers of motivation, such as money or learning or promotions, it is helpful to understand how individuals differ in their motivation archetypes. Think of motivation like dating—each of your team members has a unique combination of what they like and are looking for in terms of how they are motivated. And just like a yenta or, better yet, Tinder, your role as a manager is to match your team member with their motivation preferences.

> **To motivate your team, understand what uniquely drives each of your employees.**

Remember when you were nineteen, sitting in your Psych 101 lecture hall and learning about Maslow's hierarchy of needs? If you don't remember because Psych 101 was your 9:00 a.m. class on a Friday morning, I'm happy to remind you. The idea behind Maslow is that every human has a basic set of needs, and the more basic needs (e.g., shelter or food) must be satisfied before higher-order needs (e.g., self-actualization) can be met.

But here's an even harder question: Do you remember learning about McClelland's needs theory? Coming twenty years after Maslow, psychologist David McClelland explored a different set of innate needs that each of us has.[1] He studied how the basic human need for *achievement*, *power*, and *affiliation* impacts how an individual is motivated, particularly in the work context. Each of us is driven by a combination of these three needs, and most of us are primarily motivated by one type. For example, I might primarily be motivated by the need for achievement, though elements of power and affiliation also play a role in how I am motivated. Back to the dating analogy—it's not an either/or scenario ("My match must be either kind or smart"); rather, it's a dominant preference scenario ("I must have a partner who is very kind, and it's important that he is somewhat intelligent, though he doesn't need to be a nuclear physicist with a side hustle as a MacArthur Genius Fellow").

So, to be a great manager, it's helpful to understand McClelland's three needs, what the dominant need is for each of your team members, and how to structure work, provide praise, and reward performance based on that dominant need. If the dominant need of your team member is not met, they are likely to be demotivated at work. And when a team member is demotivated at work, they are less productive, less fulfilled, and ultimately at risk of leaving their job.

Let's go through each of McClelland's need types using three hypothetical employees: Katie, Mary, and Laura.

KATIE THE ACHIEVER

Katie has a strong need for *achievement*. She is motivated by setting and accomplishing goals. Katie likes to see progress and likes to receive regular feedback along the way. She is drawn to work where success is clearly accomplished through effort and merit. Katie also loves hiking, French wines, and athletic builds.

What's the best way to manage Katie?

- Promotions matter a lot to Katie, as they are a highly visible signal of upward progress. Make sure she understands how and when a promotion can happen.

- Give Katie projects where outcomes can be attributable to her efforts. She likes projects that are challenging but not so challenging that luck has to have a big part in the project's success.

- Make sure Katie has clear goals for the quarter or the year. Work with Katie to set those goals and celebrate them when they are achieved.

- Praise Katie's completion of tasks and recognize her specific contribution to accomplishing the task.

MARY THE POWERFUL

Mary's dominant need is *power*. She is motivated by competition and the ability to influence others. Mary likes having the ability to exert control in situations and is driven by the desire to have responsibility and sway. Mary thoroughly enjoys winning arguments and enjoys having status or prestige in her job. Mary also loves brunettes, competitive sports, considers herself a bit of a foodie, and will never turn down an invite to play a game of blackjack.

What's the best way to manage Mary?

- To reward work done well, increase Mary's responsibility and ownership over projects. A huge reward for Mary would be having management responsibilities over an individual or a team.

- Praise Mary when she comes up with the right approach or is correct about a decision. Validate the impact that Mary's ideas and work have on a decision or project outcome. Shoot an email (and bcc or cc Mary) to a senior team member praising her—that's going to be super motivating.

- Give Mary projects that have a competitive tilt (e.g., sales goals).

- Note that at offsites or company picnics, Mary will crush the recreational softball game or friendly team-building contests. She will approach building a marshmallow tower the same way she will approach beating out a competitor for a sales contract.

LAURA THE AFFILIATOR

Laura's dominant need is *affiliation*. Laura is motivated by belonging to a group and feeling a strong sense of community in her workplace. Laura loves collaborating with others and cultivating a sense of attachment to those around her. Laura will stick around an organization because of loyalty to her team. Laura also loves the outdoors, especially winter sports; nonfiction; and brainiacs.

What's the best way to manage Laura?

- Make sure Laura feels part of the team at all times and that she is accepted by the group. Spend time building a personal relationship with Laura and creating space for mentorship. Keep your eyes open for situations where she could feel socially excluded.

- Praise Laura by sharing how she's impacted the team and the organizational culture.

- Encourage Laura to take on roles and projects that involve building relationships and engaging with different members of the organization.

Now that you know the three motivation archetypes, what should you do next as a manager? My suggestion is simple: Learn what motivates each of your team members and what their dominant need type is. Observe what gets your team members excited. Observe what types of praise resonate the most with them. Create a super arbitrary office contest and see which of your employees cares the most about winning (you'll immediately sniff out the *power* types). And just ask your people what they love most about their job and what motivates them to get up in the morning. The answer to that question will tell you a lot.

For those of you who like tactics, I like to use a motivation intake form when I have a new employee join my team (see appendix). It's a simple table that asks your new team member a series of questions about how they like to be motivated (similar to a form you would fill out at the doctor's office in the waiting room). What's magical about using this form is not the specific questions or answers that get filled out, but rather that using this form opens up a conversation between you and your team member about what makes them tick. It allows for a frank, early discussion about how they like to receive feedback and be praised, and what matters most to them in a job. It helps you to understand their dominant motivation type and removes some of the guesswork about how you can best manage your team member.

The three motivational types remind me of "love languages," the five different ways people give and receive love.[2] I find the whole concept behind love languages somewhat hilarious. Often, a relationship will end, and one of the members of the relationship will justify its ending by citing "incompatible love languages." See frequently overheard comment: "My girlfriend dumped me because I didn't get her a birthday present. But she should know that my love language is acts of service, not gifts, which is why I didn't get her one." We can use the love language theory as an excuse for not exhibiting a certain way of loving a partner. In reality, however, we want *all* types of love languages in a relationship. We want time, gifts, affection, service, *and* words of endearment to be present in our partnership. Some languages might be more important than others in terms of what we value—but ask any long-(happily)-partnered person if you can get away with using only one love language and forgetting about the others.

That's how I think about motivation. Each of our team members has a dominant motivation need. And it's important to know that type and tailor your management style to meet that need. But motivation—like relationships—is a complex beast. Our teams will be motivated by a combination of things. We can't focus on one way of motivating and ignore the others. So get to know your team members and what makes them tick. A great manager tailors how they motivate each of their team members.

> Motivation—like relationships—is a complex beast. Our teams will be motivated by a combination of things. We can't focus on one way of motivating and ignore the others.

TL;DR

- Each of us is motivated by a mixture of three basic needs. Most of us have a dominant need that primarily drives how we are motivated.

- Understanding one's dominant need helps to understand what is motivating to the individual, and specifically how to structure work, provide praise, and reward performance.

- The three needs are achievement, power, and affiliation. Someone with a deep need for achievement is motivated by setting and accomplishing goals and showing progress. Someone with a deep need for power cares about their ability to influence and compete. And someone with a deep need for affiliation cares about their community and being liked by those around them.

- What's the best way to figure out your team members' dominant needs? Start by just asking them. You could also use a motivation intake form to help facilitate a conversation around motivation.

- The three needs are just a starting point for understanding the complex topic of motivation.

CHAPTER 7

GOAL INTERRUPTED: THE GOOD AND THE BAD OF SETTING GOALS

little while ago, I was on a coaching call with a marketing manager from a growing start-up. Kim was a phenomenal manager—empathetic, pushed her teammates in a supportive way, and was great at prioritizing and structuring the work her team needed to accomplish. Kim had been struggling with how to be more strategic with her team. On our call, Kim shared a huge revelation that she had had that week: Her marketing team had a set of yearly goals, but each team member didn't have a set of written goals that laddered up to these functional goals. She observed that the operations team in her company had a large, detailed spreadsheet that meticulously outlined each team member's goals, and that this team was praised for sharing clearly what each team member was tasked to achieve. Kim figured out how she could be more strategic: more goals. Kim then excitedly talked through how her team was going to spend the next few weeks developing a similar spreadsheet of detailed goals.

I completely understood Kim's giddy anticipation of her plan. But I also expressed a bit of concern: How would these goals be used and monitored over the course of the year? What behaviors would these goals drive? If the company-wide goals pivoted to respond to the market, how would these team members update their goals? Would this goal-setting exercise end up being just that—an exercise that takes a lot of time and effort but doesn't actually help guide the team's work? Would these goals be motivating to the team?

My conversation with Kim was by no means unique. Every year—often in December or January—our organizations get into a tizzy about goal setting for the upcoming year. We talk about setting company goals, stretch goals, key performance indicators, individual goals, objectives and key results, SMART goals, big hairy audacious goals, and many, many other types of goals. Every organization I've met is obsessed with goals. Goals make us feel safe. Goals make us feel organized. Goals make us feel successful. Goals make us feel like we're heading in the same direction. Goals make us feel like there is a tiny bit of order amidst our typical chaos. Like Kim, we get excited about creating a new set of goals with the hopes that these goals might solve our challenges of coordinating and prioritizing work or motivating our teams.

Yet I'm sure you've experienced the wacky effects of goals. Have you ever set a goal, achieved it, and then been rewarded with . . . more work? Which meant the following year, you made sure you didn't achieve the goal until the very end of the year? Or have you set a goal, achieved it earlier than expected and then coasted along because you already hit the mark? Or perhaps you've scrambled to achieve a sales goal by the end of the year, even though it really wouldn't matter if the sale closed on January 1? Or your team set a goal around revenue but ignored profit or operational efficiency? Or you spent a whole bunch of time setting a perfect list of goals, never to look at them again?

As a manager, you are going to help set goals for your employees and your teams. Goals help to motivate your team members, guide action, and encourage persistence. Goals are an important part of expectation setting, which I talked about in chapter 1, and an important part of individual development planning, as I discussed in chapter 3.

But despite the use of goals pretty much everywhere, goal setting is a nuanced tool that can harm as much as it can help. Goals, when poorly used, can overly stress employees, drive unethical behavior, induce the opposite outcome of what you actually want, demotivate a team, and frankly, just waste a whole bunch of time. So to be a great manager, you need to help your team members develop goals that motivate, use those goals effectively, and understand when goals *just don't matter*.

> **To be a great manager, help your team members develop goals that motivate and understand when goals just don't matter.**

Let's start first with discussing what makes an effective goal. Oodles of research has shown that great goals have the following characteristics:[1]

- Difficult but not impossible. That means your team can realistically achieve the goal, but the goal is challenging and pushes your team.

- Specific and clear. "Do your best" as a goal is far less effective than "hire six engineers."

- Time bound. Goals are much better when they have a clear deadline.

- Incorporate feedback mechanisms. That means that it's clear how an individual is tracking toward achieving or not achieving the goal.

- Commitment and buy-in from the team. When your team member sets their own goal, there is a greater commitment and desire to achieve that goal.

Pretty simple, right? Goal setting has become so prevalent that many of us have been setting these types of goals since kindergarten. We don't think twice about putting together goals and working toward them.

But what's the downside of goals? I mean, they're just notes on paper or on a PowerPoint slide, so how bad could they be? Let's discuss.[2]

WHAT MAKES GOALS SCARY

WHEN GOALS DRIVE THE WRONG BEHAVIOR

First and foremost, goals are scary in that they can inadvertently drive the wrong type of behavior on your team, and in extreme circumstances, drive behavior that might be unethical.[3] I was once on a leadership team, and we had an annual goal of a $20 million revenue target (we had to sell $20 million of consulting projects). Well, what do you think happened? We sold a whole bunch of projects without taking into account how much it would cost to deliver those projects just so that we could hit the goal. We would sell a $500,000 project that would then cost us $600,000 to deliver. But our goal was around revenue, not around profit. Guess what? We hit the goal and then had to lay off a whole bunch of employees. Not exactly a great outcome.

Some organizations get so focused on hitting a goal that they push ethics aside. Wells Fargo incentivized its employees with a goal to open as many accounts as possible. The bankers, in trying to hit that goal, opened a bunch of credit card and bank accounts without customer authorization. According to authorities, "Employees used fraud to meet impossible sales goals."[4] So *technically*, the bankers achieved their goal, but the company ended up with a three-billion-dollar fine and a reputation of being super-duper sleazy. Uber got itself into a similar predicament: In its company goal of beating the competition *at all costs*, Uber deployed tactics like Greyball, a fake version of its app that evaded law enforcement. Uber suffered significant reputational damage, and faced a federal inquiry about this practice, and Greyball was another piece of evidence that resulted in Uber's founder, Travis Kalanick, being pushed out of the company he started.[5]

WHEN GOALS ARE TOO SPECIFIC

When you put together a goal that's too specific and focus on trying to narrowly achieve that goal, you may lose sight of the bigger picture. I see start-ups do this a lot—we put a goal for our employees to sell X number of contracts, yet we miss the bigger picture of building a sustainable organization. We sell the contracts, but fail to think about profitability, operating efficiencies, or other important attributes of growth.

WHEN GOALS MAKE US MYOPIC

Goals can prevent you from seeing additional opportunities or areas of innovation because they are outside the bounds of the goals. Goals can blind us: it's important to allow ourselves the flexibility to pivot, try something new, and take a risk, despite a goal being in place. I find it crazy that many fast-growing organizations set annual goals (and insist on sticking to them) despite the fact that the organization is likely going to change drastically in the next few months. The serious risk for a start-up is when the goals prevent it from changing course in order to respond to a competitor or a shift in the market.

The COVID pandemic that started in early 2020 provides an extreme example of this phenomenon: companies that insisted on keeping the goals they set in January of 2020, despite the change in the whole world a few months later, couldn't react as quickly as those companies that allowed themselves to throw away their January goals and start afresh given the new and wild context.

WHEN GOALS MULTIPLY

When you set too many goals, you do this *very* human thing of focusing on the easy goals and ignoring the harder ones. I call this the to-do-list phenomenon: You write up a long list of things to accomplish and immediately focus on the really easy ones you can cross off (e.g., "brush my teeth"). We focus on meaningless tasks and don't prioritize the important goals that are most critical to our success.

HOW WE APPROACH GOALS
(MAPPED TO A FLAWED 2X2 MATRIX)

	EASY	HARD
URGENT	Stuff I Do That Makes Me Feel Like I've Been Super Productive	Stuff That I May Attempt to Do If I Have Time After I've Done All the Easy Goals
NOT URGENT	Stuff I Do to Procrastinate	Stuff That I'll Put on My To-Do List Next Month and the Month After That...and So On (But Never Actually Do)

WHEN WE MISS GOALS

Goals end up being completely demotivating when we don't hit them. I'm sure you've experienced that really stinky feeling when you *just* missed a goal. For example, your goal was to sell twenty new contracts this year, and you end the year at eighteen. You feel like you failed. This is the idea of loss aversion, a concept we will discuss more (and illustrate) in the next chapter. In the goal-setting world, loss aversion means that coming in right *under* a goal hurts a heck of a lot more than the positive feeling of coming in right *over* a goal (now think about how no one really cares if you came in over your contract target and sold twenty-one contracts). Instead of being a motivating force, the goal makes you feel like a huge loser.

Okay, I have been the Debbie Downer of goal setting far too long. Your goal as a manager is to help your team members be motivated, grow, develop, and be challenged in their jobs. Goals can help you do that. So, to use goal setting for the good that it can bring, remember to:

1. Think *really hard* about what behavior the goal will encourage and what will happen when the employee hits the goal.

2. Give lots of feedback along the way as folks look to achieve their goals. Build mechanisms and structures that bring goals into day-to-day work as opposed to being words in a document that you pull up once a quarter.

3. Don't set wild stretch goals and then punish failure, especially if there is a chance that your team may use behaviors (including things like working too much) to achieve those goals.

4. If you're setting a goal, make sure it's specific, your team has bought into it, it's time bound, and it matters.

5. Think about goals as being dynamic, encourage goals to change, and celebrate when a team member bails on a goal that needs to be bailed on!

One of my favorite concepts in yoga is the paradox of effort (*abhyasa*) and nonattachment (*vairagya*).[6] The idea is that we give 100 percent to a task at hand and put in a persistent unrelenting effort to what we are doing. But the paradox—the nonattachment—is that we remain detached from the outcome of that effort. We do not orient ourselves to the results of our effort but rather to the effort itself. The yogis of 400 BCE were on to something regarding goal setting: We can use goals to motivate, inspire, and drive effort, but don't let the goals be the reason why we are putting forward that effort. Happy goal setting!

TL;DR

- Goal setting is a powerful tool that can help motivate teams and drive productive behavior.

- Goals can also create unintended consequences, including unethical behavior, a myopic view of the organization, and a failure to innovate.

- Furthermore, in start-ups, annual goals are often wildly mismatched with how the business operates: static goals don't align to a dynamic and quick-changing environment.

- When setting goals with your team members, make sure you are aware of the upsides and downsides of goals, and be okay with not using goals to help motivate and guide action.

CHAPTER 8

THE COMPLICATIONS
OF COMPENSATION

Once I was talking to a leadership team about the results of its brand-new employee engagement survey. The leadership team, very much to its credit, cared deeply about the results and wanted to discuss the areas in which the organization performed worst. Take a guess at which statement scored the lowest out of the whole survey.

"I am compensated fairly."

Yup—that's right, employees were least satisfied about pay. The leadership team immediately went into diagnostic mode, trying to understand why this score was so much lower than the others, despite salaries and bonuses being well-benchmarked and generous for the sector. I appreciated the team's commitment to fixing the employees' discontent, except that every single engagement survey I have ever been part of has this same problem.

Everyone wants to be paid more (ignoring some saint-like exceptions to the rule). Everyone thinks that they are not paid enough for their brilliant skills and capabilities they bring to the world. And everyone, when given the opportunity to anonymously tell their leaders and managers that they think they are underpaid, *will*. Heck, I'd be worried if I got an employee survey back where my whole organization responded that they wholeheartedly agreed that they were overpaid.

Cash is motivating, no doubt about it. But many managers and leaders assume that compensation is *the* primary way of motivating individuals and that, if the compensation puzzle is solved, their teams will be happy, engaged, and willing to jump through hoops as long as there is a fiscal reward on the other side. In day-to-day practice, I see this phenomenon most acutely as start-ups raise their next round of funding: the instinct when there is an influx of cash is to give everyone a bump in salary with the expectation that it will solve all of the creaks and groans coming from current employees (spoiler alert: it doesn't).

But compensation is a funny thing. Research has shown that paying someone extra to do something, in fact, may *decrease* motivation and reduce the enjoyment of doing an activity because it's challenging or meaningful.[1] Yup—you read that right—those spot bonuses you think are a great innovation to encourage your team members to work outside their swim lanes might be having the opposite effect. Or how about those referral bonuses you give employees for finding someone to work at your company? Would people work harder to find referrals if they *weren't* paid and instead thought of it as a crucial organization-building opportunity that everyone chips in to do?

> **Research shows that paying someone extra to do something may decrease motivation and reduce enjoyment.**

Compensation is an important tool in how you motivate your teams. But before you use cash as your cure-all for getting your team members fired up about their jobs, it's important to know where and why cash can wreak havoc on your organization. To be a great manager, you must know when cash is motivating. And, more importantly, when it's not.

WHAT MAKES COMPENSATION COMPLICATED

LOSS AVERSION

We get really bummed out—like exceptionally bummed out—when money we thought was ours is taken away from us. This concept, developed by behavioral economists Danny Kahneman and Amos Tversky, is known as *loss aversion*.[2] What Kahneman and Tversky discovered was that "losses loom larger than gains." For example, we get far more upset by losing $10 that was in our pockets than we are elated by finding $10 on the street. So when we expect that we'll make $100,000 at the end of the year but only make $95,000, that impacts us far more from a motivation perspective than if we expect to make $90,000 and end up making $95,000.

LOSS AVERSION: MATHEMATICALLY AND ARTISTICALLY GRAPHED

GOOD

The feeling you get when you find $10

BAD

The feeling you get when you lose $10

We should feel the same about both outcomes given that we ultimately end up with $95,000, but we're irrational humans, so we don't.

A little real-life example: We were doing end-of-year performance reviews and bonus decisions at a start-up. We had a group of about fifteen associates. Most were performing well, two or three were superstars, two were a little below the rest of the group but still solid performers, and then one associate was very much underperforming. The associates' end-of-year bonuses were about $3,000, a number we had communicated at the beginning of the year. For the superstars, we gave them 120 percent of the expected bonus, so they received an extra $600. For the folks who were a little below the rest of the group but still good performers, we gave them 10 percent less, and they received a $2,700 bonus. The severe underperformer we transitioned out of the organization. The rest of the group got $3,000.

Well, what do you think happened? The superstars, despite receiving 20 percent more than their peers, were appreciative but deflated. They were thinking: *I busted my butt all year for an extra $600?* The folks who fell a bit below the curve were apoplectic: It didn't matter that they received only $300 less than expected. The fact that money was taken away from them was infuriating. It ended up being a huge demotivator, and the time, energy, and emotions that went into managing this decision far exceeded the $300 of reduced bonus.

I'm not saying always pay full bonuses to every team member. Rather, I'm cautioning you on the impact loss aversion has on your teams!

EQUITY THEORY

We care a *lot* about what our peers make. In the 1960s, psychologist J. Stacy Adams developed the concept of equity theory.[3] Equity theory states that an individual's motivation is correlated to their perception of fairness and equity in relation to others around them. Put another way, people care more about *relative* value than *absolute* value (despite it not being economically rational). Hypothetical employee Carolyn would rather make $100,000 a year if her hypothetical office mate Luis is also

EQUITY THEORY
(OR THE IRRATIONALITY OF HUMANS)

LESS SATISFIED   MORE SATISFIED

making $100,000 a year than make $110,000 a year if Luis is making $120,000 a year. Carolyn would rather leave $10k on the table for the feeling of fairness.

Let me tell you about a time when equity theory wreaked havoc: Leah was the director of operations at a small nonprofit. When she joined the organization, she was super excited: The role was exactly what she was looking for, she was passionate about the mission, and the compensation was solid. She was making a bit more than what she made at her last role, and her salary was right in line with similar roles at peer organizations. About three months in, Selina, the executive director, started noticing that Leah was a bit disconnected from work and was being less proactive in her day-to-day, waiting instead for Selina to assign her tasks. Leah started taking every Friday afternoon off, citing work stress as the reason why.

Well, Selina soon found out the reasons behind Leah's disengagement. Leah had learned that her peer, Meg, who she thought was at her same level, was making $10,000 more than her. Leah was silently livid at the inequity between her and Meg, so she took matters into her own hands to bring a sense of equity back into the work equation. She started taking more time off and doing less high-value work. It didn't matter that her pay was exactly where it should be or that she was happy about it coming in. That's equity theory at play.

PROCEDURAL JUSTICE

The outcome of compensation decisions often matters less than the process to make those decisions. There's a concept called *procedural justice* that can be used to explain so many things in life. It's particularly useful in explaining how people react to compensation decisions. Procedural justice states that individuals are more supportive of a decision—regardless of whether they agree with the decision—when there is a high degree of transparency and input into the process used to make the decision.[4] Put another way, you'll feel better about a decision you hate when you feel bought into the process to make that decision than about a decision you actually love when you weren't bought into the process. Procedural justice is also critical to building an anti-oppressive organization, as we may inadvertently maintain unjust power structures by not sharing the process for how decisions are made but rather only sharing the outcomes.

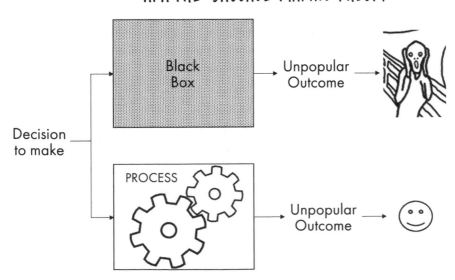

PROCEDURAL JUSTICE
AKA THE "SAUSAGE-MAKING THEORY"

How does procedural justice work in practice? Your teams will feel much better about compensation decisions if you share how you come to such decisions. For many small organizations, there isn't a huge compensation committee with a perfectly calibrated process that is 100 percent driven by data and numbers. As such, in small organizations, compensation decisions end up feeling arbitrary. I've had countless individuals complain that they feel like the CEO of their organization just waves their finger to decide compensation and that favoritism is the primary factor in these decisions. This drives team members crazy as they don't have faith that their compensation is being decided fairly.

> **Procedural justice is critical to building
> an anti-oppressive organization.**

Sharing your process, even if it is a light process with limited data, makes a huge difference. For example, you might share that you use Glassdoor benchmarks or that annually you look across all team salaries to make sure there is equity within functions or across levels. You might share that you gather a set of objective metrics as well as subjective ratings to determine bonus amounts at the end of the year.

You now understand what makes compensation potentially demotivating and what traps to avoid. We can now get into some tips and tricks around the how: How can you as a manager make sure compensation is motivating?

HOW TO CLARIFY COMP

BUILD A COMPENSATION PHILOSOPHY

Set up and communicate a compensation philosophy to your team. A compensation philosophy doesn't have to include every single little detail about how you compensate; rather, it articulates the principles you use and how those principles align with your organization's culture. For example, consider these questions:

- Do we pay slightly above market rates or slightly below, and why? Or do we aim to be aligned with our closest competitors?

- Do we use end-of-year bonuses, and what do these bonuses signal? Are bonuses typically variable or are they used more like deferred compensation?

- How often is compensation decided or altered? Often, I include here a "no negotiation" policy (i.e., individuals don't continually jockey for more money or raises outside of the prescribed process).

- How do we view non-financial compensation as part of our overall package and why? Often, management puts much greater weight on non-financial compensation (e.g., equity or 401(k) benefits) than more junior team members do, and then management gets confused when team members aren't excited about these additional perks.

Often, managers know the answers to all of these questions but never explicitly articulate them to their teams.

BE CLEAR ABOUT THE HOW

Clearly articulate *how* decisions are made for compensation and promotions. I often hear people complain that their organization prides itself on being transparent but then isn't transparent about compensation. The challenge with this statement is that individuals conflate transparency of process (e.g., procedural justice) with transparency of information (e.g., being open about what everyone in the organization makes, or how individuals rank against each other in terms of performance). Be clear about that distinction and then be clear about the process for deciding compensation. Some information you share could include what data are collected, when subjective assessments and management intuition are used, and who is making the compensation decision.

BE CAREFUL WITH BONUSES

If you tell people up front the amount of bonus they are going to get at the end of the year, you'd better (a) have the money to pay them, and (b) understand the impact that reducing that bonus will have on them. If there is any uncertainty whatsoever about the economics of your business or your team, make sure you communicate that bonuses are not guaranteed. If the economy changes, or a pandemic hits, you might need to dial back bonuses in order to save jobs or ensure the survival of your organization. Make sure your team knows this about bonuses.

Remember that even a small decrease in an expected bonus can destroy an individual's motivation (back to loss aversion). You may think that reducing someone's bonus by 5 percent at year-end will give them the kick in the butt that they need, but remember that people respond irrationally to money being taken away from them. Instead, the kick in the butt might turn into the person feeling vastly undervalued and leaving the organization.

Similarly, if you are planning to add a little bit to someone's bonus, don't expect them to be jumping for joy. Sure, people will always appreciate a boost to a bonus or a salary, but there's just as much risk of people thinking: "I busted my butt and only got a 5 percent increase on my bonus?"

INTRINSIC MOTIVATION MATTERS

Don't kill intrinsic motivation with money. And lastly, be careful about overcompensating for activities that employees may derive joy and engagement from because they are challenging and rewarding in their own right. For example, if a team member loves organizing team-building activities or another team member loves helping with recruiting, putting a monetary value on those tasks might decrease the motivation to do them.

The best example of this is referral bonuses for hiring. Often, we provide team members a monetary incentive to refer a friend or former colleague to our organization. It's great to encourage our team members to always be recruiting and recommending our organization as a great place to work. But once you attach a monetary value to this task, it no longer becomes a company-wide responsibility that is part of the organizational culture. Team members get persnickety about referrals they make that don't meet the exact qualifications of the bonus, and the organization gets resentful if they pay the bonus but then the new hire leaves sooner than expected.

Compensation is just one piece of the puzzle when it comes to motivating employees, yet it's often the piece of the puzzle that we actively get wrong. Though shocking, many times I've heard leaders say: "Why is the team unhappy? They're getting paid well." Even seasoned managers and CEOs assume that financial compensation is sufficient to motivate their teams to do great work. Not only is that *not* the case but also financial compensation might have the opposite effect on the team. So, to be a great manager, it's important to understand how compensation is perceived by your team members and how it makes them behave (both rationally and irrationally).

> **Compensation is just one piece of the puzzle when it comes to motivating employees, yet it's often the piece of the puzzle that we actively get wrong.**

TL;DR

- Compensation motivates your team, but often not in ways that are rational, and there are times when paying people more money might demotivate them.

- Be careful about taking money away from individuals or expecting a small amount of money to be a huge motivator. This is because of loss aversion—the concept that people are much more upset about losing money than they are excited about an equivalent gain.

- Individuals put much more value on relative pay than absolute pay, a concept known as equity theory. Thus, an individual would rather make less money if it means that his peers are making the same amount as him.

- We care more about how decisions are made than the outcome of the decision. It's important to clearly articulate the compensation process and ensure that your team members respect and are bought into that process.

- A well-defined compensation philosophy that aligns with your company culture and clearly articulates why choices are made regarding how you pay people will help to ensure that compensation is motivating.

CHAPTER 9

THE HEAVYWEIGHT TITLE FIGHT

The excitement was palpable. My young heart was fluttering. On my desk in a neat little box was my very first set of business cards. Printed on a rich cream cardstock, a perfect rectangle was embossed in simple yet elegant font with my company's name, my name, and my office phone number. I passed my index finger over the black lettering and turned the card over and then back again. But wait. My card had no title. No honorific of the role I played at the company. Granted, I was on the lowest rung of the corporate ladder, but the omission of any kind of title was glaring. How would people know I wasn't (*gasp*) just an intern?

Titles matter. In some organizations—like my first company—titles are de-emphasized, and senior leaders claim that they don't matter. Yet we care about titles. Titles provide us information about a person (what does this person do?); they help us categorize individuals and shape how we might interact with them (is this person senior, and as such, how might I behave?); and they carry currency and weight (I have perceived status because of my title). Often, titles are used as a motivator, as they signal progress in an organization and are a tangible way to show that we are achieving success in our roles.

But titles are only the icing on the much more complicated cake of pro-motions. Just like titles, promotions are incredibly motivating, especially for individuals who care deeply about achievement and power. Promotions signal growth and often involve increased pay and an expansion of scope and responsibility. Promotions make our team members happy . . . and as managers, we want happy teams. But how we promote and how we use titles on our teams have the potential to create a whole bunch of unintended consequences, including very *un*happy teams and managers. We often approach promotions and titles with the best intentions—we use them as a reward for work well done—but in doing so, we end up wildly regretting not being more thoughtful about both. Here's a little story that helps illustrate why.

Martin was employee number 22 at a small and mighty start-up. Martin joined the start-up as the director of operations, and in the early days was the right-hand man to the CEO. He put in place processes and systems to help the start-up grow. The CEO relied heavily on Martin and, wanting to reward both his loyalty and the instrumental work he was doing, promoted Martin to vice president of operations and then, a mere four months later, to senior vice president of operations. There were no other SVPs in the organization, so Martin's new title and level reflected his senior leadership role. Martin was thrilled with his new title and promotion.

Fast-forward six months. The company grew successfully, raised a Series B, and lots of new employees were hired. Quickly, a couple of things happened: First, new vice presidents were hired who had far more experience and skills than Martin. During the interview process, these senior leaders questioned why Martin, a relatively junior person, was an SVP and they were only a VP. It created problems in recruiting new talent who believed (rightfully so) that they were more experienced than the company's SVP, yet they were getting a lower title.

Similarly, other directors in the organization saw that Martin had been quickly promoted to SVP and demanded their own fast promotions. They rightfully pointed to their responsibilities that were similar to Martin's, yet they were merely directors. Lastly, the CEO quickly realized that the activities and responsibilities that Martin was in charge of and capable of doing weren't actually commensurate with a senior level for a larger organization. Martin was great at doing director-level activities but didn't have the actual SVP-level operations capabilities. The team needed someone with more experience and skills than Martin, but there was now no room above Martin as an SVP. The CEO needed to bring in someone above Martin, which would then mean an awkward demotion for Martin, a mere six months after getting a highly visible title change and promotion.

After much teeth gnashing and angering conversations, the CEO ended up demoting Martin back to a VP. Martin was embarrassed at losing face in front of the team, and the CEO continued to be frustrated that Martin was not even playing the role of a VP, despite having that title.

Many of you have heard of the concept of the Peter principle—the idea that individuals are promoted because of competency until they rise to a level in the organization where they are completely incompetent.[1] The Peter principle happens because we end up promoting people for the wrong reasons. We promote individuals because we don't want them to leave our organizations. We promote them to reward hard work and loyalty. We promote them for doing an awesome job in their current role. We promote them because we want to show other team members that promotions are possible.

The problem with our approach to promotions—as seen in the above example with Martin—is that we end up creating an absolute mess. In trying to make one team member happy and satisfied through a promotion and title change, we tick off a whole bunch of team members. We create problems in our ability to recruit top talent when we need it. We end up spending tons of time and mental resources negotiating titles and promotions with our team members. We end up disappointing our employees when they don't get promoted within the organization as early as they expected. And we end up cheapening promotions—they are no longer as motivating as they could be because they are taken for granted and no longer special in the organization.

The primary way to prevent a promotion mess is to use a promotion equation. I like to communicate this equation early and often to my teams, and then use the equation when I am making promotions! Here is the equation:

Let's break this down.

THE PROMOTION EQUATION

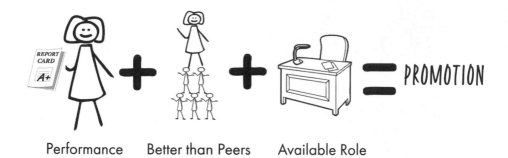

Performance   Better than Peers   Available Role

Performance means that the person is doing an outstanding job at their current role. They've mastered the competencies their role requires and are exhibiting many of the competencies of the role above them.

Better than peers means that this person—if there is a cohort of individuals vying for the same promotion—is more skilled and more successful at their role than their peers. For small organizations, this part of the equation might not hold as there may not be peers to compare the person against.

Available role means that there is a role with a new set of responsibilities and requirements that is open and needed. To be even more specific, there is a new job description, distinct from the current job description, for the role that the person is getting promoted into.

For many, *available role* is the hardest part of the equation to stomach. It means that an individual is promoted into a new role with a new set of requirements and responsibilities, as opposed to being promoted solely because they are outstanding at their current role. If there isn't a more senior role or an expanded scope needed by the organization, a promotion doesn't happen. Pay the person more money, give them a higher bonus, but don't call it a promotion if the person hasn't fundamentally increased their responsibilities and role requirements.

If a team member hasn't fundamentally increased their responsibilities, don't promote them.

Okay, so what else can you do as a manager regarding titles and promotions?

HOW TO BE THE DON KING OF PROMOTING

1. **Use the equation.** First and foremost, stick to the promotion equation and don't deviate from it. Communicate the equation to your team and communicate it again.

2. **Set promotion cycles.** Promote individuals on an annual or biannual basis. That means there is a designated period of time when promotions happen. If you promote ad hoc, your team will ask, cajole, demand, and plead for promotions throughout the year. You will get exhausted by the constant requests. In some instances (e.g., an employee leaves and you need to promote someone to fill that role or there is a change in job function), the promotion might happen off cycle. This should be an exception, not the rule. Again, communicate this to your team.

3. **Don't rush promotions.** The time between promotions may depend on the level of promotions; and as a rule of thumb, err on the side of a longer promotion cycle than a shorter one. Junior people may be more quickly promoted to the next level, as their jobs are likely to more quickly increase in responsibility. Senior team members may wait three, four, five years (or longer) to get promoted. Feel empowered as a manager to have the promotion cycle go a bit longer than you may feel immediately comfortable with. For example, it's okay if a junior team member waits eighteen or twenty-four months for a promotion. It may feel long at first, but once your organization is up and running, the time will go quickly.

4. **Yet again, set clear expectations.** Be as clear as possible with your expectations for someone's promotion. Start having conversations early and often about what competencies an individual needs to build in order to be prepared for a promotion. Work to get on the same page with your team member about their expected promotion timeline. There's nothing worse than entering a performance conversation where your team member is expecting a big promotion, and they are wildly off in terms of when they are ready for one. Start those conversations early so there aren't surprises during the promotion cycle.

5. **Use a competency matrix as a road map rather than the rules of the road.** Put together a competency matrix that outlines the competencies necessary at each level of the organization (see example of matrix in appendix). This matrix helps provide guidance to your team about what they can work on to prepare for a promotion and helps to map out their path forward. But be careful with this matrix, as some employees might interpret the matrix as a set of hard-and-fast set of rules that, once checked off, will cause them to be automatically promoted. Remind them about the promotion equation when this comes up.

6. **Party like it's 1999.** When promotions do happen, make them a huge deal. Celebrate promotions and make them special for the individual. Be clear to the rest of the team why this person got promoted and all they have accomplished. These celebrations only work if you aren't promoting people all the time.

GET THE TITLE FIGHT RIGHT

1. **Don't negotiate titles.** Don't use titles as a bargaining chip in recruiting negotiations. Often when trying to recruit a candidate you really want, the candidate might ask for a higher title if

they can't get more money. It's tempting to give them the higher title—as it's "free" to do! Resist the urge. It will wreak havoc down the line if you have folks who should actually have a lower title, whose responsibilities are of a lower level, and who are paid at a lower level but have a more senior title. It confuses the organization and ends up inflating titles throughout the team. All of a sudden, you have a team of all VPs and no managers and associates.

2. **Be stingy with senior titles.** Similarly, don't give away senior titles too quickly in the early days of your organization. When you're a small organization, use titles such as head of marketing to denote the most senior person in your marketing function, not chief marketing officer. When you double in size and you are able to recruit a marketing superstar, you'll want to have that chief marketing officer title available. It will also make it easier to bring in a CMO above the head of marketing, versus having to strip the CMO title away from your acting head of marketing. This will save you tons of heartache.

3. **Innie and outie titles are okay.** Allow for different internal and external titles. For some roles (e.g., sales) external titles matter a lot in the marketplace. Regional sales manager—as a title—might be necessary to open doors in the sales world. But make it clear from an internal perspective what the actual level and title is, as opposed to defaulting to the external title. In general, I don't care what people put on their LinkedIn profiles (within reason) as long as they are clear about their internal calibration.

4. **Be consistent.** And lastly, when possible, use consistent titling schemes across your team. For example, you might use director of operations or operations director. Equivalently, you would then use either director of marketing or or marketing director. Consistency across the organization helps especially as you scale.

I like to put together a clear set of levels and titles early on—it doesn't have to be complicated, but consistency and structure can go a long way.

Titles and promotions are incredible tools for motivating your teams. We all want to be recognized for the work that we do and want an outward sign of our progress, growth, and success. Sharing the news with a team member that they have been promoted is one of the most fulfilling actions you do as a manager. Yet few things bring as much angst and heartache to a manager as a sloppy approach to promotions. You will rue the day you promoted someone too early or gave away a title too easily. You will raise your fist, curse at the sky, and wish you had more closely read this chapter.

TL;DR

- Promotions and titles are a great motivator, especially for team members who are driven by achievement and power.

- Yet a sloppy approach to promotions and titles can ultimately hurt the person being promoted, hurt your ability to recruit other team members, and hurt your ability to motivate the rest of your team.

- The case for a promotion is made when an individual shows competence and success in their role, performs better than their peers, and when there is a new set of responsibilities and requirements (i.e., a new role) that the organization needs.

- Be clear with your team about what is required for a promotion and set the expectation that promotions won't happen quickly or willy-nilly. If possible, develop a competency matrix that helps to outline what is required at each level of the organization.

- Be thoughtful about titles, and don't use titles as a negotiating tactic; rather, err on the side of caution with titles, as it's easier to bring in someone more senior when you haven't given away all of your senior titles.

A FINAL NOTE ON MOTIVATION

Congratulations! You're now an expert on motivation. You know that individuals may be motivated by achievement, or by the need for power and responsibility, or by the desire to be part of a team. You know that money and other forms of rewards may both motivate and demotivate your team depending on how they are used. You've learned about the power of goals to motivate, and the power of goals to drive all kinds of other wacky behaviors. And you've learned that titles and promotions can inspire your team members to develop, grow, and excel at their jobs when used correctly. But astute readers will notice the absence of a very important piece of the motivation puzzle: learning.

Learning is the original motivator. Learning is the foundation of inspiration and drive. Learning powers our self-driven desire to get something done.[1] If you, as a manager, can challenge your team members, help them to explore novel activities, and expose them to new and interesting ideas—that is, ensure that they are constantly learning—you are winning at the motivation game.

But it's not that easy.

Humans are innately wired to learn. As babies and toddlers, we are constantly seeking out new experiences and stimuli. As Mr. Rogers said, children play as a form of learning and as a way to make sense of this big world in front of us.[2] When we are little kiddos, no one has to tell us to

learn—we are biologically driven to explore what's new. Learning motivates our behavior every day.

But like wrinkles, getting hungover after two cocktails, and a burn-
ing desire to go to bed at 9:00 p.m., age also impacts our innate drive to
constantly be learning. As we grow up, we no longer have to make sense
of an unfamiliar world. We get complacent and lazy about our external
environment. We lose the childlike desire to always be discovering.

So the final motivation lesson I would like to impart to you is about
learning: Great managers reignite their team members' desire to learn.

> **Great managers reignite their team
> members' desire to learn.**

What can you do as a manager to light the learning fire? Well, first and
foremost, give your teams challenging work that pushes them to learn. I
know that's not always possible. So, here is a nonexhaustive list of five
other suggestions that can help you motivate your people through learning
(roughly listed from easiest to implement to more difficult to implement).

1. **Replace the word *training* in your team's vocabulary with
   learning.** Words matter in how we think about things. Learning
   is not constrained to points in time, while training is. Learning is
   constant and ongoing, and one never ages out; training implies a
   start and end date. Learning gives agency to the learner; training
   is bound by a trainer. Learning is the responsibility of the person;
   training is the responsibility of the organization. You get my drift.

2. **Let your team silently sit in on your calls and meetings (when
   appropriate).** Let folks listen in on discussions with customers,
   vendors, and other senior colleagues.

3. **Encourage a discussion of "what you learned" after big
   meetings or big projects.**[3] This is slightly different from the
   discussion of "what we learned in order to get better next time."
   Rather, this is purely a discussion of what your team members

found interesting, novel, or intriguing about an experience. Ask questions like, "What did you find surprising?" or "What was counterintuitive?"

4. **Teach.** When a team member learns something new and great, have them teach it to others on the team.

5. **Encourage your team members to "swing on the monkey bars" instead of "climb the ladder."** We often focus on the vertical moves of work where we climb the ladder in our roles, getting promoted from one rung to another. But then there are lateral moves—moves where we take another role at the same level but in a different function or part of the organization (less of a ladder, more of a monkey bar). These lateral moves drive tons and tons of learning. If possible, facilitate and encourage lateral moves for your team members to keep them learning.[4]

In sum, celebrate learning on your team as the final piece of your motivation puzzle: encourage intellectual curiosity, encourage question asking, and encourage new points of view.

MEANING

Many years ago, my boyfriend at the time and I were strolling along a remote beach in South Africa. A woman and her dog, a Staffordshire terrier, walked past us. The Staffy was wearing a harness hitched to a big tire, yet he was happily plodding along, dragging his tire through the sand. Perplexed, we stopped the woman and asked about her dog.

She laughed and, in her deep South African accent, shared the following story. Two years earlier, she'd noticed that something was wrong with her dog. He stopped eating and moped around the house all day. Worried, she brought him to vet after vet who couldn't figure out what was wrong with him. He didn't appear to be suffering from any physical ailments. Finally, one vet recommended a dog psychiatrist. Within minutes of meeting the dog, the psychiatrist diagnosed the problem: The dog was depressed. And he was depressed because he had no purpose. Here was a working dog who didn't work. He had no reason to get up every day. The psychiatrist suggested a simple remedy: Give the dog a tire to drag around. Give him a purpose. And voilà! It worked. The dog's mood immediately improved as he happily dragged his tire down the beach every morning.

Everyone needs their tire. We all need purpose and meaning in our lives. Recent research bemoans the fact that today we are less satisfied and derive less meaning from our jobs than we did twenty years ago.[1] We strive for work that gives us purpose, that aligns with who we are and who we aspire to be, and that scratches the invisible itch of *why we are on this planet*. No longer do we stay at our jobs for forty years, and as such, we try on new roles, move to new organizations, and explore new sectors in our quest for meaning.

You now know how to effectively manage your team members' performance and how to motivate them to reach their fullest potentials. In the next step of our management journey, you will learn how to help your team members bring meaning to their jobs and their careers.

But before we get into how you manage for meaning, I want to highlight an important nuance. We often talk about *Meaning* with a capital *M*. We talk about Meaning as this grand outcome that we spend years striving for and that often is a result of much soul-searching, career switching, and very expensive therapy bills. Meaning feels binary: We either have it or we don't; and for many of us in our current roles, we just don't have it. We feel like we are constantly trying to track down that elusive Meaning and it is always slightly beyond our grasp.[2]

But there is also the small-*m meaning*. Lowercase meaning is the fulfillment, excitement, and curiosity we get from the day-to day. It's that satisfied feeling we get when we're walking home from work and we feel like we made some small impact. It might have come about because we successfully tackled a complex problem, we had an insightful conversation with a colleague, or our work was integral to a bigger challenge our organization was facing. In my very humble opinion, focusing on the small-*m* meaning will get you to the big-*M* Meaning over time, and it often is less daunting and overwhelming to focus on the little things one can do to derive meaning at work.

> We often talk about *Meaning* with a capital M. But
> there is also the small-*m meaning*: the fulfillment,
> excitement, and curiosity we get from the day-to-day.

As a manager, you are in the unique position to help your team members find *meaning* and *Meaning*. In the following chapters, we are going to explore both. We are going to discuss how to design and structure work in order to maximize day-to-day meaningfulness; how your communication as a manager impacts your team members' senses of purpose; how emotions and authenticity affect your team members' experiences; and how to use deep questions to support your team members in their broader quests for meaning.

If you, as a manager, are able to guide *just one* team member over the course of your entire career in finding their sense of purpose, you have achieved great things. The following chapters will help you help your team members find their tires.

CHAPTER 10

MAKING WORK
MEANINGFUL

Let's discuss two hypothetical employees, Kelly and Kiesha. Both are human resource associates at small companies. Read carefully as there will be a pop quiz at the end of this section.

Kelly's role is to support the human resource activities at her company. Kelly helps recruit new team members, administers employee benefits, and maintains employee files. Kelly spends each day looking on LinkedIn for potential new employees to hire. If she finds someone promising, she sends the candidate's profile over to the leadership team and waits to hear if they hire the person. She often doesn't hear if the leadership team rejects a candidate. Kelly's manager sets Kelly's schedule and defines each task she is to accomplish by the end of the day. Kelly's tasks are similar day-to-day and have been as long as she can remember.

Kiesha's role is to help her company achieve its strategic goals by ensuring that the human capital foundations—the people and processes—are strong and able to meet the needs of the changing business. Kiesha ensures that the employees at her company are cared for and supported from the first time they speak to her on a recruiting call to the day they join the company to the day they leave. Kiesha works closely with the leadership team: With Kiesha's input, the team sets the strategic direction, and then Kiesha works to figure out what activities and tasks she can do to support that strategy. Kiesha has complete ownership of these activities—such as recruiting and hiring top talent—and sees the activities through from start to finish.

And here's the quiz: Whose job is more meaningful—Kelly's or Kiesha's?

I use this example to demonstrate the following point: the same exact job—same role, same responsibilities—can be wildly different in terms of how meaningful it is to an employee. Kiesha likely derives more satisfaction, purpose, and fulfillment from her job than Kelly does, despite having the same role.

We'll examine *why* Kiesha's job seems so much more fulfilling than Kelly's later in the chapter. For now, my question to you is: Do you want to be the manager whose team members spend their days devoid of meaning, only looking forward to their fifteen-minute walk to Dunkin' Donuts and their purchase of mediocre coffee and a slightly stale cruller? Or do you want to be the manager whose team bounds into the office each day, excited about what's ahead and fulfilled by their daily activities? Let me assume you want to be the latter manager.

As a manager, you have the ability to make day-to-day work meaningful for your team members in two primary ways: how work is **structured and designed** and how work is **framed and perceived**. Let's break down both.

STRUCTURE: NOT JUST NINETIES MENSWEAR BUT A WAY TO MAKE WORK MEANINGFUL

The way we structure and design our team members' work directly influences how meaningful it is. Organizational psychologist Richard Hackman articulates a set of five design choices that make work meaningful for employees.[1] By structuring a job to focus on these five design choices, we are able to increase the sense of purpose and fulfillment someone has in their job, and in turn, we increase their motivation and overall satisfaction at work.

The five design choices are skill variety, task identity, task significance, autonomy, and feedback. Let's discuss these choices along with some handy-dandy suggestions of how you, as a manager, can curate them to help your team members find more meaning in their jobs.

1. **Skill Variety**: Work that is varied and challenging. No one wants to do the same exact thing day in and day out. When you're scoping a role on your team, make sure that the role includes diverse activities.
   - *How:* Job rotation. Can you rotate the roles on your team (even if small roles) so that individuals are constantly learning through new challenging work?

2. **Task Identity:** Work that completes a whole task or goal versus just a little piece of a task. For example, it's far more meaningful to scope the research question, conduct the research, and synthesize and present the findings, as opposed to just cleaning the data and handing that off to the data analyzer who then hands it off to the synthesizer who then hands it off to the presenter.
   - *How.* It's often more efficient to create highly specialized roles on your team (e.g., the data cleaner, the memo writer), but this prevents task identity. When possible, structure individuals' work as projects, not single tasks.
   - When possible, provide an opportunity (even if a contrived one) for people to go further along "the value chain" in their project. For example, a junior data analyst can synthesize and present their findings to the internal team, even if they won't be the one presenting the findings to the client.

3. **Task Significance:** Work that has an impact on the lives of other people. The classic example of this is the factory worker whose job is to tighten screws. He finds far more meaning when he recognizes that the screws are in service of tightening the brakes of an

airplane, and hence his work directly helps keep millions of people a year safe.

- *How*: Bring your team members closer to the *who* behind the work that you do. That might mean letting your team members silently listen in on sales calls so that they better understand how their work is impacting the client.
- Develop a frequent refrain of "how does this work serve our mission" and encourage your team to talk through how their own work serves your organization's mission.
- If possible, bring the beneficiaries of your organization's products or services into contact with your team. For example, if you manage an engineering team for a diabetes health-care company, bring an individual managing their diabetes into your office to talk about how the product has supported them. Research by organizational psychologist Adam Grant shows that bringing people closer to the recipients of their work not only helps with meaning but also improves productivity and performance outcomes.[2]

4. **Autonomy**: Having freedom, independence, and discretion in scheduling work and, more importantly, in determining how the work will be carried out.
   - *How*: Set clear expectations of output but then let your team member figure out how to achieve that output. Encourage your team member to share early and often how they are going to carry out their work, but give them ownership of figuring out how to get there.
   - If possible, allow flexibility in the hours when work can be carried out. Manage output, not time: if a team member wants to go for a run in the middle of the day or stay up late cranking on a project, be supportive of those choices.

5. **Feedback:** Knowledge of the results and effectiveness of the work that you've done. Know that feeling when you put a ton of blood, sweat, and tears into a work product, send it to your

manager, and . . . crickets? Like you hear nothing back? Not even an email that says, "Received"? Well, that's the opposite of feedback.

- *How*: First, always, under every single circumstance, acknowledge when a team member sends along work. Second, send an email that details specifically *how* a team member's work contributed to a meeting, work product, or broader goal. A note that says, "The analysis you did really helped the client to change their perspective in yesterday's meeting. It caused us to talk more about issue X," is super-duper powerful.
- Clearly show how the day-to-day work your team does aligns with the broader goals of the organization. Map out how their pieces of work fit into the organization's strategy and, when possible, share how the big projects the team did affected larger company projects or goals.

On paper, these five design elements that help make work meaningful seem simple and obvious. Yet so many managers don't structure the work and roles on their teams to include these five elements. Now that you have the structure and design down, let's move on to framing and perceiving, the second big way to help your teams find meaning.

GET OUT THE GLUE GUN— IT'S TIME TO JOB CRAFT

In our hypothetical example at the beginning of the chapter, one of the big differences between Kiesha and Kelly's role descriptions is how their work is framed. Kiesha's job describes the critical role she plays in ensuring that the business runs smoothly. It describes the broader implications of what she does—for example, nurturing other employees over their tenure at her company. On the other hand, the description of Kelly's job focuses on the discrete tasks that she does. One could argue that Kelly's and Kiesha's jobs are exactly the same, so what does it matter if Kiesha's job is framed in a more positive or broader light?

Well, our minds are powerful. By framing and therefore perceiving our jobs in a certain way, we become more satisfied with our work. We can more easily connect what we do to a broader set of objectives and link what we do daily to our long-term development goals and bigger career puzzle. This concept of reframing a job is called *job crafting*, and it was first developed by organizational psychologists Amy Wrzesniewski, Justin Berg, and Jane Dutton.[3] By encouraging your team members to craft their jobs, they will become more satisfied and find more meaning in their day-to-day work. Plus, they will feel a greater sense of ownership over their own development and learning (as we talked about in earlier chapters).

Here's how to job craft:

1. The team member starts by writing out the tasks they currently do in a "before" diagram. They group the tasks by those where they spend the most time to those where they spend the least.

2. Then the team member creates an "after" diagram that shows where they want to be spending their time, and connects their tasks to their broader motives, purposes, and strengths.

3. The team member (with support from you) identifies ways to make their day-to-day closer to the after diagram. The move from before to after won't be immediate, but there may be quick areas of change that the team member can implement.

Let me provide a little example. An executive assistant, Alex, was struggling with his career path at his start-up. His job was fast-paced and interesting, but it was starting to feel like the tasks he was doing were meaningless and offered very little room for growth. Additionally, given the structure of the start-up, it wasn't clear that there were immediate promotion opportunities for Alex. Alex felt stuck and was struggling with how to think about his role for the upcoming year. Alex went through the job-crafting exercise. Take a look at the "Before" and "After" diagrams on the following pages.

I like doing the job-crafting exercise with each of my team members. I ask them to read the Wrzesniewski job-crafting article and then have them take a shot at putting together their own before and after diagrams. It's helpful to discuss how they would like to spend their time, and it allows me to share how I think some of their tasks may connect to broader goals or motives that they might not have identified.

I also use job crafting as a group exercise—each team member takes a turn explaining their before and after diagrams. The group exercise serves two purposes: First, it enlists others to support the job crafter in how to achieve their after diagram; and second, it's a great way for the team to learn about each person's role and responsibilities. Often, I hear complaints that people have no idea what their colleagues do all day. What does a marketing associate actually do? How does a compliance manager spend her day? A job-crafting group exercise helps people to understand functions across the organization.

One final way to use these before and after diagrams? Get out the glitter and pipe cleaners and craft the heck out of your personal relationships. I have had many friends remark that they have deployed *marriage crafting* to huge success, but I won't get into those details. That's for a totally different book!

ALEX, EXECUTIVE ASSISTANT TO THE CEO—BEFORE DIAGRAM

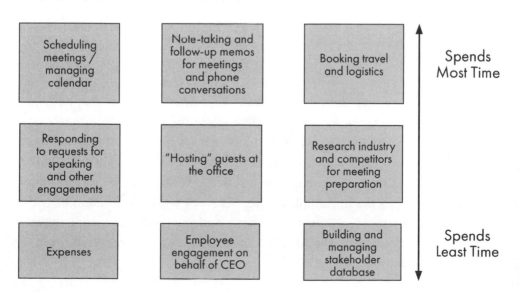

ALEX, EXECUTIVE ASSISTANT TO THE CEO—AFTER DIAGRAM

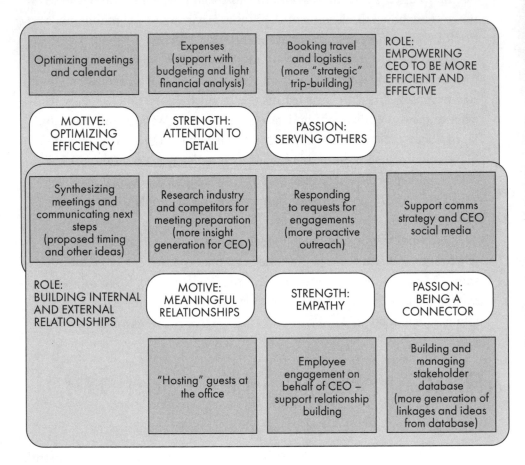

If there is one thing I want you to take away from this chapter, it's that small things make a huge difference in the meaning and purpose your team members derive from their jobs. It might be the extra five minutes you spend with your team member explaining what the board discussed at the last board meeting. It might be the email you send that acknowledges the impact of a team member's work. Or it might be the new activity that you assign to a team member in order for them to have variety in their work day. All will help in the quest for meaningful work. Happy meaning making!

TL;DR

- As a manager, you can help your team member find meaning in their day-to-day work. You can do this in how you design and structure roles, and how your team frames and perceives their work.

- There are five design choices that make a job meaningful: task significance, task identity, skill variety, autonomy, and feedback. Often, little things you do as a manager can impact those five factors.

- Job crafting is a tool used to help team members reframe how they think about their daily activities and how they align with their broader motives and purpose.

CHAPTER 11

THERE'S NO CRYING IN BASEBALL

A number of years ago, I started a new job. On my first day of work, the CEO, Trevor, and I went out to coffee to chat about my role, expectations, and strategy. As we sat down to sip our flat whites, I asked Trevor if he wouldn't mind if I shared some aspects about my life before we got into the nuts and bolts of the new job. I shared how excited I was to be working for a young, growing company in an industry I was eager to learn lots about.

I also shared my personal journey that led me to this role, a journey not spelled out on a résumé. Specifically, I shared that, two years prior, my younger brother unexpectedly passed away and that his death rocked me in an indescribable and unfathomable way. Because of this, I had made the decision to change careers and align my work more closely with my personal values. I shared that though I was fully ready, excited, and able to take on this big new role, I still was hit every so often with waves of sadness and anger. Given how closely we would be working together, I wanted Trevor to know that there would be times when certain emotions would emerge and that what I learned from my last job was that bottling those emotions up did far more harm than good. I wanted to bring my authentic and whole self to the organization— and that whole self sometimes included lots of feelings.

Trevor teared up as I shared my story, and we laughed at the thought of another employee walking by to find us both blubbering on my first day of work. But the overall message was met with openness and appreciation that emotions are a part of who we are, and whether we like it or not, emotions come into play in the workplace.

That conversation was incredibly scary for me. Since I first entered the workforce, I was repeatedly taught to always have a poker face, to never cry at work, and if I did, gosh forbid, tear up, to immediately run into a bathroom stall, cry there, and then pull myself together. As I got more senior in my career, things became a bit easier: I could shut my office door and cry silently behind my laptop. But, over time, I realized that not expressing the emotions I was truly feeling made things far worse. A slight frustration with a manager turned into simmering long-term resentment; a sadness from a personal situation took me mentally away from meetings and left the impression of me being aloof. When I became a manager, I started noticing my direct reports experiencing the same: At times, they were trying so hard to hold it together and not show anger, frustration, or even glee that they looked physically uncomfortable.

For many of us, we've been conditioned to keep feelings out of the workplace and to hide our authentic self from our coworkers and colleagues. This conditioning may be even more prominent for certain groups. We don't all have an equal social license to express our true emotions—and as such, our true selves—at work. For example, Black men may feel even more pressure and stigma to suppress certain feelings that don't align with society's expectations of them.[1] Or some women may be particularly sensitive to sharing feelings so as not to be pegged as histrionic or overly emotional. And when we don't feel safe expressing how we feel, and we spend time, energy, and worry hiding certain aspects of ourselves, our jobs feel empty, and we end up feeling exhausted.

We don't all have an equal "social license" to express
our true emotions—and our true selves—at work.

The easy solution to all of this would be to say, "To be a great manager, make sure you help your team members feel comfortable in expressing their true emotions." But emotions at work are a complicated topic. To truly be a great manager, you need to understand the paradox that emotions present in the workplace: It's important for your team members to share and be authentic with their emotions in the workplace. But emotions (both negative and positive) spread quickly, and one team member's feelings can deeply impact the rest of the team. Before I get into the *how* of managing emotions, let's first discuss the *why* behind emotions and this paradox. Why is it important to consider emotions at work?

HOW EMOTIONS IMPACT US AT WORK

EMOTIONAL LABOR

Emotional labor, first coined by sociologist Arlie Hochschild, is the mental and psychological work we do to regulate our emotions.[2] In particular, emotional labor occurs when our inward emotions don't match our outward emotions, and as such, we have to put energy and attention toward exhibiting an emotion we aren't truly feeling. For example, if I had a really bad morning and I'm internally angry, but then I have to greet customer after customer with a huge smile at my workplace, my body and mind are doing emotional labor.

Emotional labor occurs when our inward emotions don't
match our outward emotions, and we have to put energy
toward exhibiting an emotion we aren't truly feeling.

Emotional labor is an important concept to understand as a manager because it may come at a cost to employee well-being. Team members who are expected to do a high amount of emotional labor (think customer-service or client-service jobs) often experience higher degrees of burnout. So if you have a team member who constantly needs to suppress their true emotions and exhibit other external emotions all day at work, there need to be opportunities during the day for them to express their true emotions. Think about how much better you've felt (as embarrassing as it may have been) when you accidentally cried in front of your boss. You released the emotion and were then able to move on, most likely feeling a little lighter and much more able to focus on the task at hand.

During the height of the COVID pandemic, a manager, Cara, was leading a team of care coordinators. These care coordinators spent all day on the phone supporting families of individuals who were elderly, chronically sick, and at a greater risk of becoming impacted by the virus. During each call, the care coordinators projected a sense of calm, control, and positivity as they helped the families navigate their options for additional care. Cara started to notice, though, that her team of coordinators appeared far more exhausted than what their actual workload would predict (also taking into account the overall stress of the pandemic). Here's what was happening: Cara's team was doing an immense amount of emotional labor. They were projecting cool and calm all day, though internally, they were stressed, anxious, and also panicking about the health and economic uncertainty that the coronavirus was bringing. Their own families were impacted, yet call after call, they suppressed these feelings of fear in order to support their clients. Once Cara realized this, she created space at the beginning and end of each day for her care coordinators to discuss their own personal feelings. Not only did the release of pent-up emotions help her team members, but also, the team members were able to do a little less "work" by not having to hide their true feelings all day at the workplace.[3]

The easy answer to emotional labor is to ensure that your team members feel comfortable sharing their emotions all the time, and for you to create space for them to do so. But before you totally upend your organizational culture to constantly encourage the outward manifestation of explicit contempt, untethered giddiness, extreme anxiety, or other emotional states, we now turn to the flip side.

EMOTIONAL CONTAGION

Emotional contagion is the immediate and subconscious spreading of emotions from person to person. Think viral disease, where the pathogen is happiness, annoyance, or fear. For example, Renee comes to a team meeting carrying the burden of her missing cat. She's totally bummed and walks in with shoulders slumped, doesn't make much eye contact, and talks in a low-energy, slow way. Well, immediately and subconsciously, the other team members "catch" these emotions from Renee and start mimicking her behavior. The otherwise upbeat weekly team meeting feels like a total drag and a total downer. The team leaves the meeting and spreads this emotion to other people they come into contact with throughout the day. Renee has no idea that she was patient zero in spreading a bummed-out feeling throughout her organization that day.

Emotional contagion is important to understand because often we don't know *why* the team meeting feels the way it does or *why* our close-knit working group is overly giddy. When we don't understand why we are behaving in a certain way, we may attribute these behaviors to the wrong stimulus. We might assume our team thinks an idea is bad or that an interview candidate is not qualified because our team is in a negative emotional state.

It's also *especially* easy to spread emotions in a group when you're the person in charge. For example, when you walk into a room with a huge smile on your face, guess what, your team will likely smile back. If you're openly anxious about the future of your company, no doubt your team will pick up on that and quickly become anxious too. As a manager, you can help stop or encourage the spread of certain emotions.

Interestingly, some emotions are particularly helpful for certain tasks. A team experiencing joy may be better at a creative brainstorming task than a neutral team. A team that is feeling a little down in the dumps might actually be better at completing a task like running through budget numbers or editing a report.[4] Perhaps the spread of sadness is appropriate when a team member is suffering a loss. Or perhaps the spread of "ticked-off-ness" is completely unhelpful to the task at hand, and therefore you stop it in its tracks.

So the downside of encouraging your team members to share their emotions all the time is that it might subconsciously impact your other team members in ways that may or may not be helpful. That's the emotional paradox. Here are some ways you can support your team members in bringing their emotions—and authentic selves—into the workplace while also being aware of the risks of contagion.

FLEXING YOUR EMOTIONAL MANAGER MUSCLE

ASK WHAT'S-UP-BELOW QUESTIONS

Build into your management practice (e.g., your one-on-one meetings with your team members) questions that ask how your team members are truly feeling. And be truly interested in a response other than "fine." The functional medicine doctor, Mark Hyman, calls these the *"What's up below?"* questions—questions that go a level deeper into how someone feels.[5] In making these questions a regular occurrence as opposed to just asking them when you think something might be off, you'll start to make your team feel comfortable sharing how they are truly feeling. Recognize that some team members might not ever be comfortable sharing how they feel deep down—and that's okay too!

> Build into your management practice questions that ask how your team members are truly feeling. And be truly interested in a response other than "fine."

MODEL IT

Model the behavior of being open with *your* genuine emotions with your team members. I once cried in front of a graduate class I was teaching. We were having an intense group discussion, and it reminded me of loss and grief in my own life. My raw display of emotion gave permission for the students to do the same. And what was amazing is that it appeared to give permission for the class to exhibit a wider range of emotions—the students felt more comfortable sharing unbridled joy as well as sadness in the classroom.

MAKE YOUR TEAM AWARE OF THE LINGO

Share with your team the concept of emotional contagion. Encourage your team to share in a meeting if they might be off and help your team to realize that they can help stop the spread of an emotion that might be spiraling out of control. Better yet, do a quick mood check at the beginning of team meetings. Get into the habit of doing a quick round-robin checking-in with how people are feeling at the start of a meeting.

RUN TOWARD EMOTIONS—THE GOOD, THE BAD, AND ESPECIALLY THE UGLY

Celebrate successes and milestones that have wonderful positive emotions, and openly acknowledge the situations that bring about strong negative feelings. Run toward emotions—good or bad—when they pop up on your teams. Often, we are so petrified of upsetting someone (especially at work) that we avoid a heartfelt "I'm sorry." Guess what—it's far worse to avoid the negative emotions than to accidentally trigger them.

LIKE A BAD DYE JOB, EXPOSE THE ROOTS

When it's appropriate, ask *why* to help your team members understand what is driving their emotions related to work. For example, if a team member expresses that they are anxious about the upcoming merger, ask why. They might be anxious because they're nervous about their job, or nervous that they might get a new manager. A feeling of anger could actually be a feeling of loss or fear. A feeling of uncertainty could actually be a feeling of excitement. Getting to the root cause of an emotion can allow you to better support your team member in navigating that emotion.

One final note: A special case of emotions at work occurs when there is a situation that evokes different emotional responses from different members of your team. Our workplace is a social system and we feel the same social pressures to conform, to maintain our status, and to not be cast as outsiders as we did in seventh grade.[6] Therefore, your team members will be pressured to feel a certain way that is aligned with the rest of the team so as not to be perceived as being different.

For example, a company I was working for was acquired by a larger organization. Some team members were thrilled—there were going to be new career opportunities and access to extensive resources. Other team members were bereft—they were anxious about the uncertainty ahead, grieving the past, and fearful that they might lose their jobs. Team members felt extreme pressure to conform to the emotions of others in the group. Thus, many team members hid their true emotions because they wanted to be seen as brave by their peers, not anxious or scared. And it can go the other way—a colleague I know was uncomfortable sharing how energized he was by a work crisis: He had adrenaline coursing through him and was ready to dive in to solve the problems at hand. The rest of the team was anxious and uncertain. He felt shamed into conforming to the team's negative emotional response to the crisis and therefore didn't share his authentic feelings.

Managing emotions as a manager is no easy task. Emotions are complicated. People are complicated. The last piece of advice I want to leave with you comes from a church that was at the end of the street where I grew up. Every week, the church would put up a new quote on a little billboard on its lawn. My favorite?

"Feelings are everywhere. Be gentle."

TL;DR

- Emotions are a tricky topic in the workplace—we are often encouraged to hide our feelings, often to the detriment of bringing our authentic selves to our jobs.

- Emotional labor occurs when the inner emotions someone feels don't match the outer emotions someone is expected to express. Lots of emotional labor can cause stress and burnout at work.

- Emotional contagion is the immediate and subconscious spread of emotions between people. Emotional contagion is particularly impactful on a team, where one little negative emotion can quickly create a collective negative emotion of the whole team.

- As a manager, you should be aware of these concepts, and make sure your team members can express their true emotions, but also protect the organization from quickly spreading emotions.

- In sum, feelings are everywhere. Be gentle.

CHAPTER 12

TALK IS NOT CHEAP

Years ago, I joined a big data start-up at its inception. There were only five employees, including a junior research associate, Erica. At the beginning of our start-up's life, the starting five, including the CEO, would sit in our temporary conference room together and scheme, strategize, and execute on building our organization. As a group, we discussed big decisions (who do we want to be as an organization) and little decisions (what should the color scheme be of our launch invitation), and Erica, despite her less senior stature, had a voice in these decisions. Any big news that the CEO learned immediately made its way to the rest of the team. Information flowed freely. Work was meaningful.

Fast-forward six months. We hired more team members, some more senior than Erica. We structured a formal leadership team that met separately from the rest of the organization to discuss big decisions. Work became more specialized, and Erica now focused specifically on her job tasks. Erica was no longer part of the conversations about office design and company events. The trajectory of our organization was exactly what we anticipated and desired and we were all excited about the team's growth. Erica knew being jammed in a tiny conference room together was not going to last forever, and she welcomed so many of the changes that our growth brought along.

But Erica still experienced a huge feeling of loss. Not a loss because her role became narrower or because she wasn't in leadership meetings, but a loss because she was no longer "in the know." Previously, big news about a new investor or partnership was immediately shared by the CEO. Erica knew about the people we were hiring and knew what day a new employee was joining. She was never surprised by information trickling in from an outside source—she was close to the information, and communication of big things was quick and seamless. Now communication was much patchier. Information that used to be instantaneous might take a week to get to the rest of the team. And information Erica used to be privy to was now private. Erica felt disconnected and distant. Work no longer felt meaningful.

Anyone who has ever been part of a growing organization is familiar with some version of this story. The loss of being close to information is one of the most painful parts of an organization "growing up," and one of the biggest challenges that early employees grapple with. The antidote to this pain is easy: communicate early and communicate often. Yet as managers in fast-paced environments, we get really busy and forget to communicate. Or we think that the information we could share isn't that important. Or we think that we *are* communicating plenty and that we are sharing enough with our teams.

Well, I hate to break it to you. You probably aren't communicating to your team members enough. And this lack of communication is hurting your team and making it harder for your team to find meaning in their work. To be a great manager, you must communicate.

I am going to share tips, tricks, and nuances of how to ensure you are sufficiently communicating to your team. But if you're short on time, my prescription for how to be great at communicating as a manager can be summed up by the following two quotes:

The single biggest problem with communication is the illusion that it has taken place.
—George Bernard Shaw

Repetition never hurt the prayer.
—Anonymous

So the first rule of good communicating is simply to make sure you are actually communicating. And the second rule is to overcommunicate. Repeat the point you want to get across. Then repeat it again. And repeat it one more time.

> The first rule of good communicating is simply to make sure you are actually communicating. And the second rule is to overcommunicate. Repeat the point you want to get across. Then repeat it again. And repeat it one more time.

Okay, now, let's talk a little bit more about *why* communication matters in making people feel connected to their roles and their organizations, and some more tips on *how* you can communicate well as a manager.

THE ART OF COMMUNICATION

IT ALL COMES BACK TO EXPECTATION SETTING

Remember chapter 1 of this book? We learned about the importance of expectation setting as a manager. Well, communication is all about expectation setting with your teams. The challenge with communication is that, absent of clear expectations, team members expect there to be communications about everything in the organization, and then end up being sorely disappointed when reality doesn't match those expectations. I like to set communication expectations in three buckets:

> Communication is all about expectation setting with your teams.

- Let your team know what you commit to **actively communicate** to them (for example, big decisions coming out of leadership team meetings or how promotions are decided).

- Let your team know what you will **not communicate** to them (for example, the detailed notes from a board meeting or if someone in the company is on a performance improvement plan).

- And let your team know the information that you will **passively communicate** to them; that is, information they can ask you for or seek out themselves (for example, the notes from a new client meeting—you may not actively communicate this to your team, but there is a shared drive where team members can access them if they're interested).

A word of warning: So many start-ups I know pride themselves on being transparent. The CEO touts transparency as a cultural value and talks about how the company openly communicates all of the important information to the team. CEOs love the idea of an egalitarian culture where the leadership team has nothing to hide. This is all well and good in theory, but in practice, the cultural value of transparency often ends up being an epic disaster. That's because there is some information that is not appropriate to share with the whole company. The team complains when they don't get the full, transparent picture when someone exits the company (and for legal or ethical reasons, the leadership team can't provide the full picture when someone is fired); or the team complains that the company is not openly communicating the equity amounts of different team members. A recent example was a CEO whose employees became livid with her because she didn't immediately share that she was in talks about acquiring a smaller company. Given the organization's culture of transparency, the employees expected to be privy to a very confidential transaction that could have easily been derailed if any of the one hundred employees shared the information with a friend or family member.

Not all information can be communicated. Better to set expectations from the get-go that some information will not be communicated, and that employees cannot have full transparency into every part of the organization.[1]

WORDS MATTER

The second component of communication I want to talk about is the power of words. The *way* you communicate matters: If done well, your communications have the ability to bring your team closer to your organization's mission and bring a greater sense of meaning and purpose to your employees' day-to-day lives. Psychologists Nira Liberman and Yaacov Trope developed construal-level theory, which states that how we talk about things—that is, whether we use specific or abstract language—impacts how emotionally, psychologically, and socially close we feel toward something.[2]

> **Your communications have the ability to bring your team closer to your organization's mission and bring a greater sense of meaning and purpose to your employees' day-to-day lives.**

For example, if you are communicating to your operations team about a new product launch that the engineering team is working on and you use specific, vivid language ("The new version, called Alpha Pi, has three different features from the last version."), your team will feel emotionally closer and bought in to that launch, despite it happening with another team. If you speak in generalities and abstract terms (e.g., "The launch is better than the last version."), your team will feel much more distant from what's happening. They might not care whether the engineering team is successful (and that might be okay, depending on what you want for them).

Similarly, through communications, you can help your team feel connected to the mission of your organization and derive meaning from that connection. In chapter 10, I spoke about the power in sharing a specific story of who our work affects. In communicating, the more we rely on stories about specific individuals, the more connected our teams will feel to their work and the more meaning they will derive from it.

This focus on the individual is often illustrated with a phenomenon called *compassionate collapse*.[3] We have a harder time building empathy for large groups of people harmed by a disaster (e.g., the mass casualties of a tsunami) than we do for a single individual who is harmed (e.g., the deceased toddler who was a Syrian refugee). Compassionate collapse is present in the workplace too.

Here are a few more ways you can better communicate with your team. And remember, most important is that you just do it, and second most important is that you just do it over and over and over again.

A Listicle of How to Get Talking as a Manager

- **Weekly Email:** Get in the habit of sending a weekly email to your team that summarizes any big news for the week. This suggestion sounds super simple and really boring, but the power is in its consistency. Set a day and time and commit to sending the email. I also find that a consistent structure (e.g., an operations section, product section, people section) that you can repeatedly populate works well. It also ensures that you don't miss information that should be shared.

- **Senior Team Meeting Output:** Commit to sharing high-level bullet points from management meetings or senior team meetings. Often, our teams interpret no information as something nefarious. In reality, we provide no information because we're just disorganized and a bit lazy. Five bullet points highlighting what was discussed at a senior team meeting goes a long way in making people feel in the know and comfortable.

- **Internal Communication Strategy:** Put together a light internal communications strategy for your team. This is just a quick overview of the different communication channels (e.g., the weekly team meeting, your weekly email, the team Slack channel) and what key pieces of information (e.g., new hires starting, updates from other functions, company financials) are communicated in each channel.

- **Ask and Ask Again:** During team meetings, ask your team members if they have outstanding questions or if any information is unclear or hasn't been communicated. Again, it's a simple thing, but makes a huge difference if you build the habit of asking your team what questions they have, especially during team update meetings.

I was chatting with a coaching client, Molly, who manages a team of fifteen. Molly had spent tons of time developing a new part-time work policy, discussing it with external advisors and syndicating it with the senior leadership team. She mentioned that she had told her team about the new policy change and all that it entailed, yet team members still seemed to be unclear about and unaware of the policy. Molly was frustrated with her team. But Molly only communicated this update once during a virtual team meeting. One team member may have been about to hit Purchase on her Amazon basket; another team member may have been composing an email to a client; another team member may have been scrolling through an amazing article in *US Weekly*; and a final one may have just mentally checked out of the meeting. In Molly's mind, she had sufficiently communicated this big change. But for the rest of the team—who weren't as close to the information as Molly—they needed this policy communicated multiple times in multiple forms to fully grasp and absorb the change. So start communicating!

TL;DR

- As organizations grow, communication often suffers, and employees no longer have access to the information that they used to.

- The most important aspect of communication as a manager is to just make sure you are doing it. And make sure you are doing it often and repeatedly.

- Oftentimes, our team members struggle with our communication of information because of misaligned expectations. Clarifying what will be communicated and what will not be communicated is important.

- Our words matter when we communicate to our teams. Words that are specific can help team members feel more committed and closer to our organization's mission.

- Other ways to ensure you are communicating enough include formalizing a weekly team email, committing to summaries of key meetings, and building an internal communications strategy that the team is aware of.

CHAPTER 13

BEAUTIFUL QUESTIONS

A few years back, I was on an early morning jog with my friend Fiona. As is common on these morning runs, we were talking about life, love, and work. I was blabbing on and on about the pile of to-dos I had and the angst I was feeling about my broader work "purpose" when Fiona asked me a question that stopped me in my tracks. She asked, "What would happen if you just didn't make any career decisions this year?" I hadn't thought about that question, nor had I thought about my career as something that could be more emergent over the course of the year as opposed to mapped, dictated, and decided. I didn't have an immediate response to her question, but over the next few weeks, her question stuck with me as I grappled with an answer.

When was the last time you were with a friend or a colleague and they asked you a question that just hit you? You know, the question that made you see the world in a different light or that made you explore an area of your thinking that you hadn't thought to explore? Or the question that completely changed your perspective on yourself?

The philosopher David Whyte calls this a "beautiful question." Whyte remarks that a beautiful question shapes a beautiful mind, and that "a beautiful question starts to shape your identity as much by asking it, as it does by having it answered."[1] We can ask others beautiful questions, and we can also ask ourselves these beautiful questions. These beautiful questions help us on our quest to find Meaning.

> **We can ask others beautiful questions, and we can also ask ourselves these beautiful questions.**

As a manager, you are in a unique position to help your team members both develop new skills and grow as individuals. In past chapters, we talked about development plans and helping your team members own their own development by articulating the skills they want to build over the year. We ask our team members where they want to go and what capabilities they need to get there. We've also talked about the power of coaching your team members. During coaching, we ask questions that help your team build the muscle to work through difficult decisions. Coaching can push our team members to challenge their thinking, explore options they might not have otherwise, and see others' points of view.

But what about the power of every so often asking your team member a beautiful question? Asking them a question that might not have an immediate answer but that gets their mind turning and expanding in a way that it might not have otherwise? A question that shifts their perspective or identity in a new way? Beautiful questions can help build a deeper relationship with your team members, build trust between you and your team, help your team members be more fulfilled in their day-to-day work, and ultimately, help your team members discover their big-*M* Meaning.

> **Beautiful questions build deeper relationships with your team members and help your team members discover meaning in their work.**

Beautiful questions are impactful because they push the "answerer" in a couple of different ways. Let's explore *why* beautiful questions are so powerful.

WHY BEAUTIFUL QUESTIONS?

THE AMBIGUITY EFFECT

As humans, we hate ambiguity. We strive for certainty and structure. This constant desire for clarity is called the *ambiguity effect*, first coined by economist Daniel Ellsberg.[2] It's the tendency for humans to avoid options where the outcome is uncertain or unknown (even if the uncertain option is likely better than the known option!). Well, beautiful questions help us to override this effect. They force us to get more comfortable with responding, "I don't know," and sitting in the uncertainty of future options.

THE AMBIGUITY EFFECT

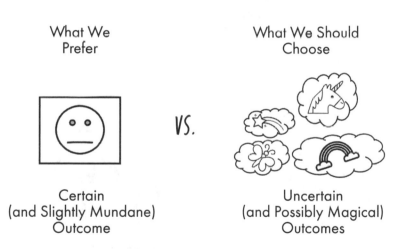

What We
Prefer

VS.

What We Should
Choose

Certain
(and Slightly Mundane)
Outcome

Uncertain
(and Possibly Magical)
Outcomes

STATUS QUO BIAS

Humans hate change. Even if the change is good, we all struggle with change. This is partly because we suffer from something called the *status quo bias*. Cognitively and subconsciously, we have a strong bias for things to stay the same. Therefore, it's hard to look outside our expected path or the prescribed goals we set for ourselves. Once we've put a path or goals in place we don't want them to change. Beautiful questions challenge us to explore change. They give us permission to think outside our paths, regardless of how well-worn or well-paved those paths are. A beautiful question lets us contemplate life if we have dropped out of med school to start a business or moved from the city we love to try something new.

> **Beautiful questions challenge us to explore change. They give us permission to think outside our paths, regardless of how well-worn or well-paved those paths are.**

STATUS QUO BIAS
AKA THE "CHANGE IS HARD" BIAS

What We
Prefer

What We Should
Choose

VS.

Status Quo

New (Much Better)
Situation

ENCOURAGE VULNERABILITY

Beautiful questions encourage vulnerability—that is, being open and sharing in a way that might feel scary or risky. Well, vulnerability builds trust, and with trust comes a whole bunch of other wonderful benefits in a working relationship (or just relationship in general).[3] When you ask your team member a beautiful question and you truly listen to the response, you show that you care about them and getting to know them in a deeper way, and in a way that might not be directly related to their current role. (NB: Beautiful questions pop up all the time when we talk about falling in love.[4] Why? Because these questions naturally build vulnerability and closeness.)

By now, you're probably convinced that beautiful questions are the absolute bomb. But your team members might think you're a little weird if you come into work tomorrow and start dropping some major beautiful questions on them without any warning. In my experience, I like to use beautiful questions in a few different ways.

First, at the beginning of the year or during periods of transition (e.g., a team member gets promoted, or better yet, *doesn't* get promoted), you can ask your team member if they would like to spend some time exploring different questions. Questions like *What three to five adjectives or phrases do you want people to use to describe you in this upcoming year?* or *What did you learn about yourself this past year that you didn't know before?* are powerful ways to kick off the new year and help your team member envision how she wants to grow. A great manager I know, Ken, takes each of his team members at various points during the year through a visioning exercise that includes a few beautiful questions for his teams to ponder.

Second, keep your ears open in your one-on-one conversations with your team members for opportunities to ask a beautiful question. Perhaps your team member is struggling with career decisions or just stuck in some area of their life. Ask the beautiful question and know that your team member might not answer on the spot or answer ever. That's okay! The point of a beautiful question is to get the brain juices flowing.

Lastly, I've known some amazing managers who share beautiful questions with their teams as a way to bring their teams closer together and gain more knowledge about each team member. Beautiful questions like *What is the single most important guiding principle that you live by? What are the primary needs, desires, and forces that drive your decisions and behaviors on a day-to-day and moment-to-moment basis?* are particularly powerful in team settings.[5]

There are endless beautiful questions to ask. Along with the questions above, here's a list of a few of my favorites to get you started, curated over the years from friends, coaches, yogis, students, philosophers, and colleagues.[6]

A STARTER KIT OF BEAUTIFUL QUESTIONS

- What are the things (people, places, activities) that make you feel truly happy? What do you not like doing or where are the places in your life where you feel drained? How can you get more of the former and less of the latter in your life?

- When in your life are you fully present? Where in your life are you hiding (areas that you are not fully present and know you can be)?

- What are your particular talents/"gifts to give" toward a solution to a particular challenge?

- What do you most need to let go of in your life? What would you be relieved to finally release?

- What would happen if you woke up in the morning and the problem you are facing is gone? How would you know that the problem was gone? How would you feel and what would you do differently without the problem there?[7]

- How much of your satisfaction is predicated (whether explicitly or implicitly) on the premise that things in your life will somehow change or evolve in the future? How distant would this assumed future have to be for you to seriously reevaluate your complacence with things *exactly as they are*?

- Would you be happy living your life as it is *right now, forever*? If not, what's missing, what needs to go, and what is in your power to do about it?

TL;DR

- Beautiful questions are questions that help you ponder life differently or think about a situation in an entirely new way.

- Beautiful questions are great at helping your team members to push against the ambiguity effect, the desire for clarity over uncertainty, and the status quo bias, the desire for things to stay the same.

- Additionally, beautiful questions help build trust between you and your team members.

- Beautiful questions can also be a great way to help build a team dynamic and build empathy throughout your team.

A FINAL NOTE ON MEANING

Dear reader, we've covered a lot of ground in these last few chapters. We've pondered the bigger questions of life and learned about our huge responsibility as managers to help our team members find meaning in what they do. You might be feeling a little overwhelmed by all the things you could start doing with your team members. Well, there's one more thing to put in your meaning tool kit that I've failed to mention.

Sometimes, the most powerful way you can help your team member find meaning is by . . . zipping it. As managers, we often forget the power of taking a team member out for coffee, asking them how they're doing, and then being totally quiet. We forget how meaningful it is to feel truly listened to and to have the space to talk about whatever is on our minds.

> Sometimes, the most powerful way you can help your
> team member find meaning is by . . . zipping it.

There are many times when we overengineer our management. We spend hours and days devising the best way to solve a performance problem. We plot out, using game theory and logic trees, why our team member might be demotivated or behaving in a certain way. We create elaborate sessions and questions to uncover the root cause of a team member's feelings. But what we often fail to do is first ask our team member what they are experiencing, and then actually listen to their response without judgment or expectation.

Okay, so here comes the complex, research-backed guide on how to take your team member out to coffee and create space to listen to what's up in their life. Here we go:

- Step 1. Ask your team member to get coffee.

- Step 2. Ask them what's going on and how they're feeling about things.

- Step 3. Shut up. (Like truly shut up. Don't follow up with additional context. Don't jump in after five seconds of silence. Just shut up, embrace the silence, and listen—they will eventually talk. Trust me.)

Done.

Sometimes, meaning is made through a beautiful question. Other times, it's an elegantly designed job that allows for feedback and autonomy. Meaning can come from an authentic emotional experience in the workplace, or a set of communications that are honest, compelling, and frequent. And meaning can come from a four-dollar almond milk latte (well, probably five dollars by the time this book is published), a simple "How are you?" and the invitation and space for a response.

PART II

MANAGING A TEAM

HIRING AND FIRING

I keep a never-again journal. In this journal, I list the things I will never ever, under any circumstances, do again as a manager. This list is a reminder of those mistakes that I've made in the past that feel catastrophic at the time but then quietly slip into forgotten history, only to be made again.

What's on this list? Never again will I promote someone before they are actually ready and deserving. Never again will I treat titles cheaply. Never again will I assume a start-up's equity value is going to grow exponentially (and make financial decisions based on that assumption). Never again will I allow for a vague, ill-defined vacation policy. Never again will I not properly kick the tires on an organization I am joining.

But the longest section of my never-again list is overwhelmingly about building a team. Never again will I not properly vet someone before hiring them. Never again will I take a chance on a candidate despite red flags and just hope things work out for the best. Never again will I wait to fire an underperformer.

The never-again list about building a team is so long because these mistakes come back to haunt us in an epic way. A bad hire will make your life miserable. A bad hire will make you wish you had stuck with your childhood piano lessons and became a concert pianist who never has to manage anyone. A bad hire will make you regret not raising your hand for the project in Siberia where you had no direct reports. A bad hire will make you yearn for the days when your only *serious* responsibilities were doing the occasional latte run and coordinating your office's March Madness bracket.

Enough said. Hiring and firing are darn important. Hiring and firing are some of the most important things you will do as a manager. In the upcoming chapters, we will talk about how to hire and fire *well*. We will discuss why we are usually terrible at selecting which candidates are going to be successful in a role. We will discuss how critical it is to incorporate new people onto your team in a thoughtful and methodical way. And we'll discuss breaking up with your team members in a way that's more "conscious uncoupling" and less celebrity divorce gone wild.

CHAPTER 14

INTERVIEWING 101

Congratulations! In your role as a boss-person, you now have the power to build a team. And as Spider-Man once said, "With great power comes great responsibility." The responsibility of recruiting new team members is one of the most important and impactful activities you will do as a manager. Hiring the right people makes life wonderful—full of rainbows and butterflies and unicorns. Hiring the wrong people makes life a nightmare. You'll spend countless hours ruing the day you let your standards slip or took shortcuts with your interview process and ended up with a total dud of a hire.

> **Hiring the right people makes life wonderful—full of rainbows and butterflies and unicorns. Hiring the wrong people makes life a nightmare.**

But doing a great job hiring is just as much about the impact it has on you and your team as it is about the impact it has on the candidates you recruit, interview, and bring onboard. Yes, we want to find a great team member as a result of our recruiting efforts, but we also want to make sure that the interviewing process is a worthwhile, compassionate, and equitable experience for those involved. As preached by the self-enlightened every-where, it's "about the journey, not just the destination." So let's talk about the interviewing journey.

First, a little story. A few years back, I was unceremoniously rejected after a final round job interview. To make the rejection sting a little more, I had to wait five weeks to hear if I had gotten the job, despite two *very* nicely worded emails kindly inquiring about the status of my candidacy. And to make matters even worse, the rejection email I received included the patronizing line: "Perhaps you can come back in for an interview two years from now, once you have gained more experience."

This was a job to be a yoga teacher. To be precise, a substitute yoga teacher. And to be even more precise, a substitute yoga teacher at a rock-climbing gym (not even a real yoga studio). Needless to say, I was furious, then hurt, then indignant, then vulnerable, then resigned. What right did these yoga interviewers have to tell me that my down-dog instruc-tions weren't good enough and needed two years of honing despite the fact that I *already taught yoga*?

But after the smoke cleared and I wisely told myself that perhaps the opposite of yoga is utter rage at other yoga teachers, I realized what a lesson this audition provided me. I was reminded of the importance of the interview process from the perspective of the job candidate. No matter how far along we are in our careers, it feels crappy to be rejected, and little things—like the timeliness of an interviewer's response—still make a huge difference in how you feel about an organization. And it was a reminder that when you're the one interviewing for a role, twenty-four hours feels like a brutal eternity, but when you're the one doing the interviewing, twenty-four hours feels like a snap of the finger.

Exceptional managers have empathy for the candidates they are interviewing and deploy the tools necessary to find, assess, and hire the best talent.

To be a great manager, you must create and run an interview process that ensures both phenomenal outcomes and a positive experience for all. Exceptional managers have empathy for the candidates they are interviewing and deploy the tools necessary to find, assess, and hire the best talent. How do you do this? You build a structured, consistent, bias-free interview process that you and your team use every single time you hire someone. Every. Single. Time.

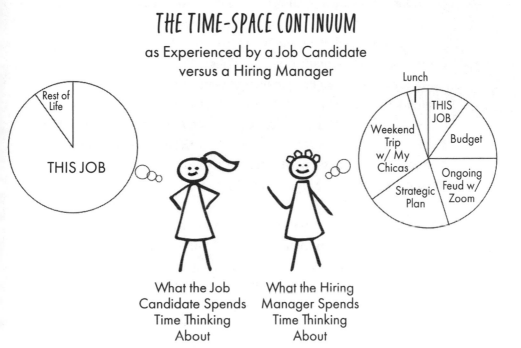

THE TIME-SPACE CONTINUUM

as Experienced by a Job Candidate
versus a Hiring Manager

What the Job Candidate Spends Time Thinking About

What the Hiring Manager Spends Time Thinking About

Let's talk a little more about *why* it's so important to build and stick to a structured, consistent interview process.

WHY A STRUCTURED, CONSISTENT INTERVIEW PROCESS?

1. **It's science, baby. (Social science, that is.)** Research shows when you use a structured interview process, you get better output.[1] That is, the people you hire through a structured

process are more likely to be successful in their new role. So if you want to have a team of people that end up stinking at their jobs and making your life miserable as a manager, go for it. Continue to use an all-over-the-place, random interview process.

2. **You hire for what you and your organization** *actually* **need.** Having a structured process forces you to clearly articulate *what* you want in a candidate and be precise about how you determine if the candidate actually has those skills. Many times, we fall into the trap of changing job requirements because we meet a candidate that we love. We convince ourselves that we *must* have this person in our organization, even though they may not have the qualifications we need. We then end up with someone who can't actually do the job we need them to do (or is overqualified), and we end up having to hire an additional person.

3. **You reduce implicit biases.** We are all biased, whether we know it or not. As we will discuss at length in the next chapter, humans have a tendency to like people who remind them of themselves. We penalize people who do not look and act like us, and we run the risk of not properly assessing those people because of superficial differences. When we don't have a clear process, we may be letting implicit biases come into play and unknowingly perpetuating an oppressive and racist system.[2] A structured process also forces us to examine *why* someone is "not a good fit." Is it because the candidate doesn't "look" like what we want a salesperson to look like? Or is it because they don't have the skills or experience that are required to be successful at the job?

4. **The candidates—regardless of whether they are hired—have a better overall experience.** First, even if you know a candidate is the perfect fit right off the bat, they should still be put through the whole process. It's important for the candidate

to feel like they are getting thoroughly vetted and are able to fully demonstrate their skills. A great candidate who is not put through a full, challenging process may question if their future team members were sufficiently screened and assessed (and, will consequently be strong and competent coworkers).

Second, when you have a clear interview process in place, with protocol for timely follow-up, there's less of a chance that a candidate will slip through the cracks or get accidentally dissed because a work fire drill comes up or life just gets busy. I know that you, dear reader, would never purposely take forever to get back to a candidate, but we run the risk of doing so when other activities become higher priority.

5. **In the long run, it will make your job** *so much easier*. You don't have to re-create the wheel every time you hire someone. Your team is all on the same page about the approach and the expectations of what role they will play in the process. You get great at interviewing and get better and better at assessing quality in a candidate. And the cognitive load of worrying about where things stand with interviewing a candidate is off your mind—it's now on paper and clearly managed.

Okay, so now onto how you create a great interview process.

A STEP-BY-STEP GUIDE TO CREATE A GREAT INTERVIEW PROCESS

1. **Outline each step** of the interview process (from how you will screen candidates to give an offer). For each step, include the following:
   - who is in charge of the step and who else on the team is involved and in what capacity. For example, who is responsible for writing the job description?

- the timing between each step that you will commit to (time to get back to candidates, ideal time between interviews).
- what materials are needed to support each step (e.g., background check, phone screening).

2. For each new role, write a list of **the must-haves for the role** (that is, the capabilities that the candidate absolutely needs to have to do an awesome job at the role) and the nice-to-haves (the additional characteristics that are helpful but not mission critical).
   - You want to test and hire a candidate that has your must-haves, but you might have to compromise on some of the nice-to-haves. Be crystal clear about what these capabilities are and create the right interview guides to test those (see step 3).
   - For example, you're hiring a director of finance for your team, and you absolutely need someone who has extensive, strong experience in financial planning and analysis (FP&A) and building forecasting models for your team. It would be good to have someone who also has a background in the biotech industry, but it's not a top priority. If a star FP&A candidate comes from the tech industry, that's better than hiring a candidate who is mediocre at FP&A and has a health-care background. Hire for strengths.

3. **Create interview guides** for every type of interview and for every role you are interviewing for.
   - Be thoughtful about what questions will result in responses that actually help you assess the quality of the candidate. Often, we ask questions about what a candidate did (their experience) instead of how successful the candidate was at doing something (the *quality* of their experience).
   - Structure the interview questions as behavioral. "Tell me about a time when your leadership abilities got called into question" is *far* more useful than "What's your leadership philosophy?" We will talk more about why these behavioral questions are so important in the next chapter.

- Ask the same questions to every candidate interviewing for a certain role. For example, if you are interviewing five candidates for a role as an executive assistant, those five candidates should all be asked the same questions. This allows you to compare answers across the candidates (and reduces bias).
- Force every interviewer to stick to the guide. This does not mean you and your interviewers have to be robotic and cold. It does mean you may need to practice being conversational and friendly while sticking to a script.

4. Create a **written assessment or presentation** that the candidate can spend time preparing that further tests the capabilities from step 2.
  - The best way to assess a candidate's ability is through their actual work product. That's hard to do in an interview, so try to come as close as possible to a simulated activity that will show you what their work product is like.
  - Examples include a written memo that analyzes a policy or provides a recommendation; it could be a PowerPoint deck that outlines a strategic plan for a new product; a presentation to your team that helps you to understand the candidate's public speaking and facilitation skills; or a financial model that tests analytical and modeling abilities.
  - In those instances where the candidates submit the assessment, you can reduce your biases further by assessing the submissions without knowing which presentation belongs to which candidate. It provides another opportunity to be objective in your assessment.

5. Develop a **structured way of collecting interviewer feedback** quickly after each interview; and make sure the feedback is structured around the key capabilities that are being tested (not just "What did you think about Eric?").
  - Insist that the team doesn't discuss the candidate until each interviewer has had a chance to put their feedback in writing.

(Why? There's a concept called mental contamination—which is when your opinions are subconsciously influenced by others around you whether you like it or not. We'll talk more about this concept in chapter 19).
- Make it crystal clear who the decision maker is in the different steps of the interview process. If you are just looking for input about a candidate but the person giving the input doesn't have the power to nix a candidate, make sure that is known. Or, on the flip side, if anyone has the right to voice no for a candidate and that eliminates the candidate from the running, make that known.

I'm not guaranteeing that every interview process will be perfect and that snafus won't still arise. When I think about epic interview fails, I think back to an interview I had with a small start-up in Cambridge, Massachusetts, on a cold December day. It was a morning-long interview, primarily with the CEO of the organization. About halfway through the morning, I asked to use the restroom. The office had a single bathroom whose door opened directly into the open-plan space. Well, I apparently didn't properly lock the door, and the CEO walked right into the bathroom, and our eyes locked. Not only did shock and horror register on both of our faces, shock and horror registered on the faces of the employees seated near the bathroom who I could clearly see from my vantage point (or "disadvantage" point). After I pulled myself together, I then had to go back to my interview with the CEO. For the rest of the interview, the two of us were more awkward than a bunch of sixth graders during a coed health class. I didn't get the job.

Dear reader, I hope you never go through an interview process (from either side of the table) that is as mortifying as what I experienced. But I do hope that you follow the principles I laid out in this chapter as you go forward in building your team. Your organization may already have a structured, codified interview process that you follow every time you set out to hire someone. But if you don't, there is a template in the appendix that will get you started in creating your own structured interview process. Happy hiring!

TL;DR

- It stinks when you get rejected from a job, but it builds empathy for when you may have to reject candidates as a manager.

- The best way to make sure candidates have a great experience and you get great outcomes is to have a structured, consistent interview process.

- A consistent interview process reduces implicit biases you have, and it makes your life easier as a manager.

- A consistent interview process also ensures that you are treating all candidates with respect and empathy regardless of whether or not they get the job.

- So put all of the steps of your process in writing, determine decision makers, be clear about what you want in a candidate, and create interview guides and assessments that actually test what you are looking for.

- Always lock the bathroom door. Always.

CHAPTER 15

WHY THE AIRPORT TEST STINKS

I've no doubt convinced you that a structured interview process is the way to go. But even in using a structured interview process, you may still end up relying on the popular method of assessing a candidate called the *airport test*. You may have used this test to determine whether someone is a good fit for your organization—that is, whether they align with your organization's culture and way of being.

Let's step through how the airport test works.

What we say: I want to hire someone who I wouldn't mind being trapped in the Detroit airport with for eight hours during a mid-February snowstorm.

What we mean: I want to hire someone who reminds me of my friends and who I could have a beer with.

What we say: We should hire people who are great cultural fits and embody the culture of the organization.

What we mean: We should hire people who remind us of ourselves, because we are fantastic at our jobs and are completely aligned with our organization's culture; therefore, candidates who are like us will also be fantastic at their jobs and aligned with our culture.

THE AIRPORT TEST:
GREAT FOR A NEW BEST FRIEND!

I love podcasts!

I went to summer camp in Maine!

My college boyfriend knows your cousin!

So do I!

No way! Me, too!

Wow! What a small world!

THE AIRPORT TEST:
REALLY CRAPPY FOR A NEW TEAM MEMBER!

What do you mean you don't know how to use Excel?

How come this project is so disorganized?

You seemed so competent at the airport!

Let's talk about this week's episode of Radiolab!

I had a project due?

That's because I'm great at chatting, people watching, and drinking on the company expense account!

As we discussed in the previous chapter, it's really hard for us to objectively hire people. Why? Because we like people who are *just like us*. This particular cognitive bias is called the *affinity bias*, and it simply means we gravitate toward people who look and act like us—and we do it subconsciously. (In the appendix, I provide an activity you can do with your team that vividly demonstrates our affinity biases in action.)

> **It's really hard for us to objectively hire people.**
> **Why? Because we like people who are *just like us*.**

You think you like a candidate because they're easy to talk to, competent, and would be fun to be around in the office. Nope. You like them because they remind you of you and you are inherently egocentric. You think you're great at your job (and it's hard for you to see your own flaws), so you end up gravitating toward people who remind you of yourself. And the scary thing about hiring people because of how much you like them is that many organizations actually encourage it, calling it "testing for cultural fit" or the gosh-awful airport test.

Even with a structured, consistent interview process, you still run the risk of hiring people based on your gut feel, intuition, and liking. You end up not seeing significant flaws in a candidate's abilities because you're having so much fun talking to the interviewee about your shared love of podcasts and Trader Joe's. You don't end up hiring for what you actually need on your teams and in your organization. You end up creating an organization that lacks diversity of all kinds (which can result in groupthink, limited innovation, and a lack of inclusivity, and can perpetuate the status quo in society).

But it's scary to throw gut feel to the wind and only rely on objective data. It's scary to start to use a structured interview process and override our gut instincts about individuals (because our guts are biased and flawed). We still want to know if the candidate is a good person, shows humility, cares about others, and is great at being part of a team.[1] How do we build into our structured interview process a way to test values and whether we want this person in our organization?

In comes the behavioral interview question. As we discussed in the prior chapter, step 3 of the structured, consistent interview process is the development of interview guides. These interview guides aim to ask questions that accurately and thoroughly help you to understand if a candidate has the capabilities you are looking for. The interview guides don't just contain any old questions. Great managers use behavioral questions to determine whether a candidate is going to be a great team player and is aligned with the characteristics you deem important in your organization.

Because a wise person once said, "Repetition never hurt the prayer," let's do a quick recap of why structure and consistency are important when interviewing, and why behavioral questions totally rock.

- *Why structured?* Because it forces you to ask all of the questions you've set out in your interview guide that are meant to test a holistic picture of the person. It prevents you from going down an interview rabbit hole for twenty minutes about the mutual friend you and the candidate both know and how great that person is.

- *Why consistent?* Because you ask the same question to every candidate, allowing for true comparison across candidates. And it helps to reduce your subconscious biases that may cause you to "go easier" or show favoritism to a candidate.

- *Why behavioral?* Because these questions—which follow the structure of "tell me about a time when . . ."—get at what people actually did in a situation as opposed to what people think they would do in a future situation.

Here are some behavioral interview question examples:

- *Typical Question:* "We have a feedback culture at our organization. How comfortable are you with receiving and giving constructive feedback?"

- *Behavioral Question:* "Tell me about a time in the last six months when you gave constructive feedback to your boss. What would you have done differently?"

- *Typical Question:* "Do you disagree often with your manager? How do you approach disagreement?"
- *Behavioral Question:* "Tell me about a time when you had to disagree with your manager. What was the disagreement, how did you handle it, and what was the outcome?"

Savvy interviewees are really good at making stuff up and talking in platitudes. It's easy to say, "Yes, I disagree with my manager all the time. I approach disagreement with equanimity and from a place of data." It's much harder to finesse a recent example. When you ask for a specific example, candidates end up self-censoring less and telling you *exactly* how they behaved in the situation. And lots of folks will be proud about how they behaved, despite the fact that you are actually looking for a different type of behavior.

I remember an interview I conducted where the interviewee proudly talked about how incompetent her boss was and how she successfully got him fired. She thought this was a huge plus because she single-handedly did all the work of the boss and her team anyway. In the interviewee's mind, she was sharing about how competent she was. In my mind, I was assessing humility, team orientation, and ability to work in difficult contexts (and she had none of those characteristics).

Hence, what you end up learning from a series of behavioral interview questions is how someone *actually* operates in the work environment:

- You listen to how someone behaved in past situations that will likely arise in their future work environment.

- You can assess if their work style (e.g., conflict averse or conflict seeking) is in line with what you need in the role and on your team.

- Additionally, you can assess how team or self-oriented an individual is. When you ask about past successes, you can listen for how much someone talks about their team versus their own accomplishments.

- You can listen for if the person is constantly blaming others for difficult situations in their past or if they take ownership and are proactive about challenges that they faced.

The more you conduct these types of interviews, the better you will get at picking up distinct cues and clues that let you know what this person would be like to work with.[2] In the appendix, I've included a table of some of my favorite behavioral interview questions and what values these questions test.

Not all candidates are familiar with behavioral interviewing and may not have prepared for an interview littered with tell-me-a-time-when questions. Some organizations send a candidate a little packet before their interview that highlights topics that will be covered in the interview (and sample questions). This approach helps to create a more level playing field and reduce biases: Some individuals have different mental processing times, and the extemporaneous interview questions might be more challenging or more anxiety inducing for one individual than another (though not reflective of how well someone could do a job). Mixing off-the-cuff questions with questions about topics the candidate knows are coming is a powerful approach.

I also like to explain at the start of the interview that I will be asking a series of behavioral interview questions, and what I am looking for in an answer: a brief overview of the situation, the action the candidate took, and the result of that action. I remind the candidate to be concise and direct with their answer, and that I might interrupt or ask for clarity during the interview. Again, I do this to level the playing field. A candidate who is very nervous may ramble, or they may ramble because they don't have an answer to the question. I am direct and set expectations up front so that I can differentiate between the two and make sure I am accurately assessing the candidate.

So, happy interviewing. And obviously the right answer to the airport test is "I would never be stuck in an airport with someone for eight hours. At the first blush of a delay, I would head to the airport Sheraton, raid the vending machine, and watch *Bravo* until my plane took off."

TL;DR

- It's hard to hire well because we let our biases come into play. In particular, we fall for the affinity bias, which means we are drawn to people we like because they remind us of ourselves.

- Hiring people based on if we like the person creates two significant issues: first, we reduce diversity of thought, experience, and background in our organizations; and second, we fail to bring in the skills or the competencies we actually need.

- To reduce this bias and test if someone has the characteristics that you need in your organization, a structured, consistent, behavioral interview is helpful.

- Behavioral interview questions ask how a candidate actually approached a past situation and how they acted and reacted in that situation.

CHAPTER 16

THE NEW KID ON THE BLOCK

I adjusted my poly-blend lady's blazer and pushed my hair back behind my ears. I quickly did a food-in-the-teeth check in the reflective elevator door, and furtively sniffed beneath each arm. I took a few deep breaths, tried to bring my racing heart down to an acceptable rate, and walked into my new office. I was nervous, anxious, excited, and scared. What if my coworkers didn't like me? What if I said the wrong thing on my first day? What if my boss realized that he hired the wrong person and that I wasn't qualified for the job? What if my elevator teeth check had failed and my spinach breakfast burrito was on full display?

This was my first day as an executive at a start-up, though the feelings that were bubbling up were almost nostalgic. The feelings were reminiscent of my first day at a new high school, where I hid in the school library and ate lunch out of fear of rejection from my classmates. The feelings were also reminiscent of starting my first job out of college, my first day at my business-school internship, my first day at my post-business-school job, and oh wait, my first day at every other job I've ever started.

Being the new kid, no matter how far along you are in your career, is scary. We have fears of fitting in, eating alone at lunch, and being accepted by those around us. Starting a new job means new colleagues, a new manager, and a new set of roles and responsibilities, some of which may be out of our comfort zones. Full stop—that's downright petrifying.

What's even scarier is that we are justified in our fears of being rejected or not fitting in when we join a new organization or team. As humans, we are hardwired to be suspicious of outsiders. A new person is different from the insiders based on the simple fact that they are not part of the current in-group. Subconsciously, newness creates distance, which risks trust-building, and in some instances can evoke stereotyping.[1] This effect may become even more pronounced when the new joiners have noticeably different characteristics from the in-group (e.g., age, race, gender). Plus, whether we admit it or not, there may be a sense of competition. Our new coworkers may be silently sizing us up: Is this person a friend or a foe?

There is a lot at stake for your team after you've hired an individual and they are about to join your clan. For starters, greater solidarity and a sense of belonging with a team reduces the likelihood that a team member will leave. There's more trust and collaboration when people feel welcomed and fully integrated. And when a new person doesn't feel integrated, there's the risk of conflict, competition, and lots of turnover.

> **When a new person doesn't feel integrated, there's the risk of conflict, competition, and lots of turnover.**

Dear reader, you may be thinking: *I don't have to worry about assimilating new people into my team. My team and I ran an impeccable interview process, our team foundation is rock-solid because of our focus on psychological safety and norms, and we are all just the friendliest bunch of folks around. We would never make a new joiner feel unwelcome or excluded.*

Well, to that I say: You have one chance to get it right when a new person joins your team. You have one chance to make sure not only that the new person feels welcome with open arms but also that they feel productive, integrated, and assimilated in less obvious ways. Often, the friendliest teams are the worst at onboarding. They assume that their welcoming demeanor is sufficient for someone to have a positive joining experience. But to be a great manager, you need to onboard new team members thoughtfully, consistently, and thoroughly, and you should leave nothing to chance when you welcome a new person onto your team.

So let's get onboarding right. At first glance, many of these onboarding activities I highlight seem deceptively simple or intuitive. But when you have a large team, everyone is going a mile a minute, and you might be onboarding multiple people at once, it's easy to forget to do even the simple activities.

WHAT TO DO SO THE NEW GAL DOESN'T FEEL SO NEW

BUILD A CHECKLIST

First and foremost, build an onboarding checklist for your team and stick to it. Your organization might already have an onboarding protocol; if it does, build on it for your own team. Like medical charts in a hospital, checklists help to ensure that nothing gets forgotten and that everyone knows their role to play in the process.[2] New people coming in immediately feel more comfortable when they know that there's a clear process for getting the information they will need to be successful. It's not on the new person to run around the office the first week chasing down questions about technology, office norms, and whether the fridge contents are off-limits. (A past coworker of mine, Kaitlyn, still recounts the time when she found out that the top shelf of the office fridge wasn't communal until after she had been eating someone's yogurt every day for five months. Don't put your new joiners in that mortifying position.)

I like to structure onboarding checklists as "activities to be done a week before the person joins," "first-day activities," "first-week activities," and "first-month activities." Put together the checklist and stick to it every single time someone comes on board. In the appendix, there is an onboarding checklist template that you can adapt and use for your team.

DON'T UNDERESTIMATE THE POWER OF A COFFEE

For your first meeting with your new team member, take the person out to coffee and get to know them as a person. Give the person space to share what they are excited about, what they're nervous about, and anything else personal that they didn't have a chance to share in the interview. I know the first day will be busy, but make the time. It will be worth it.

START IMMEDIATELY TASKING

When a new person joins, immediately task them with a project that has a deadline about two weeks out. This gives the person the opportunity to work on something meaty right off the bat and fills the time in between getting-to-know-you meetings and required trainings. Often, we are so worried about overburdening the new person that they end up sitting around the first few days, awkwardly twiddling their thumbs, wishing they had something to work on. A specific project also boosts confidence, helps them to understand how the team works, and makes the person feel immediately useful to the team. (Bonus points if the assigned project requires that the new person interact with other groups in the organization.)

ENLIST OTHERS IN THEIR SUCCESS

Get your current team quickly invested in the new person's success. Many organizations assign a new joiner a buddy to answer questions throughout the week, take the new joiner to lunch, and be a friendly face in the building. But even more powerful than a buddy is assigning the new joiner to work on a joint project with another team member. Working on a collective goal is one of the best ways to build a cohesive team, so it helps your current team in feeling comfortable and close to the new person as well. You could also task existing team members with running parts of the onboarding process, including trainings, to help get them invested in the new joiner's success.

Organize a lunch for the newbie with a different member of your team every day for the first week (this includes virtual lunches if you're remote). Make this part of your overall team culture and emphasize its importance over and over again to your current team. Remind your team of their role in welcoming a new team member and that onboarding is a team effort (not just the responsibility of the hiring manager).

MORE COFFEE

At the end of their first week, take your new team member out to coffee again and ask them for reflections from the week, anything that is still unclear, or any outstanding questions. Ask for feedback about the onboarding process and what you and the team could do to improve it (and enlist the newbie in helping out in the future). And most importantly, *share* information about yourself during this meeting if you didn't have an opportunity to during the first meeting. Show some vulnerability as a manager, and your new team member will feel even that much more comfortable with you and the group (and you'll start to build the foundation of trust).

Dale Carnegie in *How to Win Friends & Influence People* talks about the way that your dog greets you at the end of the day—with sheer, unadulterated joy—and how that makes you feel when you walk in the door. When we're welcomed by others in the same way—with energy and excitement simply because we showed up—we feel great. Onboarding can create that same feeling in new people. Build discipline and process in how you onboard, and those little things you do will make a huge difference in how accepted your new joiner feels. And a simple, heartfelt "Thank you for joining the team. I am so excited that you are here!" can go a really long way.

TL;DR

- Joining a new team or new organization is scary and anxiety inducing.

- Existing team members may also be wary or distrustful of new individuals joining their team or organization.

- Great managers build disciplined process and structure around onboarding new people into their teams and organizations.

- An onboarding checklist that is used consistently for every single new hire ensures that nothing is forgotten when someone joins; it also brings comfort to the new joiner that they're not missing critical pieces of information or technology needed to be successful at their job.

- Additionally, managers should make sure to take the new joiner out to coffee for the first meeting; immediately assign a project that takes about two weeks to complete; and enlist the rest of the team to support the new person's success.

CHAPTER 17

BREAKING UP IS HARD TO DO

Let's talk about the three ways you can break up with someone: (1) ghosting, (2) sending a vague yet rambling text message, or (3) for the really courageous folks out there, having an awkward conversation in a coffee shop neither of you will ever go back to.

Breakups in organizations can feel just as brutal as the Wild West of dating. Like dating, a breakup in an organization typically happens in one of three ways: (1) a team member quits and leaves for greener pastures, (2) a team member is let go because of performance issues, or (3) a team member (or multiple team members) is let go because of organizational reasons (often called a layoff or reduction in force). And like dating, regardless of whether you are dumped by your team member, or you do the dumping, breakups are hard and often make everyone involved feel bleh.

As a manager, you will spend countless hours discussing, worrying, counseling, coaching, and communicating exits from your team. The first time you ever have to fire someone will feel monumental. Over time, you may get more comfortable having the difficult conversation with a team member about their exit, but you'll still spend just as much time, care, and anguish managing their exit as you did for the very first person you let go.

This chapter comes full circle: I've discussed interviewing, hiring, and onboarding your team members, and now, dear reader, I must discuss how to break up with a team member. Great managers know how to manage when people leave.

Great managers know how to manage when people leave.

Let's assume that you have a team member, Kalli. You have done all the hard work for Kalli to stay part of the team—you've given constructive feedback, you've coached, you've provided development opportunities, and you've put her on a performance improvement plan. You've agonized over the decision about what to do, and you've put forth all of your best efforts to get things to work with Kalli. But you've decided that you need to let Kalli go. You thought the decision to let Kalli go was the hard part—but it doesn't end there. Why is it hard for you and your team when a team member exits?

When the decision is made for a team member to leave, things get hard in two keys ways.

First, as a manager, you care about communicating openly with your team. Yet employee exits frequently run counter to our desire to be transparent: Often, there are components of the exit that can't be communicated to the team to be respectful of the person leaving (e.g., you might not want to tell your whole team that Kalli was let go because she fudged her expense account numbers). But that often leaves your communication around the transition feeling incomplete or purposefully elusive to the rest of the team. Especially in small organizations and start-ups where everyone knows everyone else, the official discussion about someone leaving is wholly unsatisfying. You want to tell your team more, but you can't, and thus, when you communicate an exit, you end up feeling like you are damned if you do, damned if you don't.

Second, when folks leave, it's often bittersweet, awkward, and at times, acrimonious. When a team member quits, the team left behind can have feelings of resentment (especially if the quitting means more work for the team members left behind), and feelings of rejection ("Wait, we are not good enough for you?"). When a team member is asked to leave, that team member may harbor anger, and may share that anger with other remaining team members. And the team remaining may then have their own fears about if they are next—an involuntary exit creates feelings of insecurity for other team members, whether those feelings are justified or not. There are lots of emotions during a breakup, and as a manager, you may have a lot of people who are mad at you, despite your intention of doing what's best for your team members and your organization. Managing the mad is hard. Full stop.

Let's now get into the details. These are not going to be the details that a legal team or human resource manager would provide you. I will not get into the policies or procedures around exiting (which could fill an entire book). Rather, I am going to discuss how to manage your team, the exiting team member, and yourself for the three different types of breakups.

Breakup Type 1: A team member quits

- When a high-performing team member quits on you, you feel awful. You feel betrayed, you feel like you couldn't do enough to get them to stay, or you feel like the team member was ungrateful for all the opportunities you gave them.

- Resist the urge to feel betrayed. Instead, celebrate when your superstar team member quits for an awesome new job. As a great manager, you encourage and nurture growth in all of your team members. If that growth needs to happen outside of your team or organization, that's okay. In fact, that's great.

- Here's why: When an exceptional employee leaves for an incredible new role, it signals to the rest of your team and your organization that you are a talent magnet. You find great people, help them grow, and then launch them into awesome things. In turn, you'll attract more great people, and the cycle continues.

- The remaining team members might be nervous that the team will break when a high performer leaves. But when a team shows time and time again that it is stronger than a single high-performing team member, it becomes an even more powerful signal of the strength of (and desire to be on) your team.

- Communicate to your remaining team members why you, as a manager and as an organization, encourage top performers to leave. Be open about what it means for the rest of the team. Talk positively about the contributions that the person leaving made to the team and celebrate them when they depart.

- Of course, we have team members who quit who are not top performers. They might quit because they don't like the team culture, are ready for a change, or a host of other reasons. Still, celebrate them when they depart.

- Work to ensure that a team member quitting is never a surprise, especially because this allows you to appropriately plan team resources, future head count, and coverage for work. To make sure you aren't surprised by a departure, commit to one-on-one check-ins that, over time, build trust and facilitate bigger questions about career and desires; and commit to a development plan process where your team member highlights their long-term goals (and you can have the honest conversations about whether your organization can help them achieve those goals). And your team member is more likely to be open with you about their plans for departure when they see how supportive and encouraging you've been of past team members' departures. They won't be scared to share.

Breakup Type 2: You let a team member go because of performance (or other) issues

- Most importantly, when you decide to let go of a team member because they are not performing, make sure that decision is a result of a thorough and open process to help the team member improve. By the time the decision is made, the team member is fully aware that they have not been performing well over time and they have been given sufficient assistance to improve (see performance improvement plans, chapter 5).

- In the conversation with the team member when you relay the information that they will be let go, state the decision clearly and unequivocally. Again, this information should not be a surprise to the team member, but it's important to be crystal clear what is happening. Often, in difficult conversations we "overtalk" and bring in lots of unnecessary information that confuses the other person in the discussion.

- If the person being let go is open to it, work with them to develop a clear communication plan to share with the rest of the team. Often when a team member is fired, they are embarrassed and scared about what their coworkers will think of them. Share how you will communicate their departure to alleviate some of those concerns.

- Show tons and tons of empathy and generosity. Losing a job is scary, disorienting, and a huge blow to one's identity and self-perception. If possible, provide the person transition time to start job searching and provide as many resources as you can to support that.

- Communicate the exit to your team. Acknowledge that this person is leaving and share all that they have contributed to the organization and the team. Some team members may know that this person was a poor performer; others may have had no idea and may have thought this person was doing an exceptional job. Thus, the person's leaving may come as an absolute shock.

- It's important to convey that you worked with the person over many months to support their performance. You want to ensure your team members that decisions like this are not arbitrary or ad hoc: there is a structured, clear, and thorough process to support performance. You want your remaining team members to feel comfortable.

Breakup Type 3: The reduction in force (the "RIF")

- If a number of people on your team or in your organization are being laid off because of economic concerns or a strategic change in the organization, there will likely be a detailed process with employment lawyers to determine the who and the how.

- As discussed previously, it's important to show massive empathy and generosity for the team members who are laid off. You may be constrained by what you can offer or the terms of the exit, but you can seek to be helpful as a resource, a sounding board, and a network.

- An RIF is scary for the team members left behind because they wonder if they will be next and wonder about the overall health of the organization. If you are embarking on an RIF in your organization, cut deeper than necessary. That means err on the side of laying off more people than you think you immediately need to, in order to ensure that you only need to do the cut once. Continued cutting (e.g., getting rid of ten people, then two months later getting rid of another five, then three months later getting rid of five more) is the worst scenario. Your team will remain in a perpetual state of fear and uncertainty and absolutely no work will get done during those periods of uncertainty. Rather, cut deep, and cut once.

- Focus your communication to the rest of the team on certainty, stability, and how the organization is going to move forward. Share how else the organization is addressing its economic or strategic changes (e.g., is the organization also cutting back on expenses or travel?) and share, if anything, what your team can do to help. When the team has some agency—that is, they feel like they have a little bit of control in helping the situation—they will feel much less helpless when this change happens.

- With your reduced team, this may be a good time to revisit team-building exercises that I will talk about in chapter 18. You may want to set new norms and spend time re-forming your team in this new context.

I know. I know. Discussing exits is a bit of a bummer. But they'll be a frequent part of your life as a manager. Here are a few more general tips for managing any type of exit:

- **Develop a detailed transition plan** that outlines the responsibilities of the person exiting and who will be taking over those responsibilities, including managing the person's direct reports. List everything. There have been times when an individual was let go and the team realized afterward that they weren't aware of something that the person was doing that was mission critical.

- **Have all the details nailed down before you communicate** the exit to the rest of the team. The team will want certainty—they will want to know when the person is going, who is taking over the individual's responsibilities, and if there is a replacement. Have that information for them.

- **Don't hide exits and expect people not to notice.** Be open with your team when people leave and encourage them to ask questions. And be comfortable saying "I don't know" or "I'm not able to fully answer that" in response to those questions. It's better to acknowledge an exit than take the sitcom route where a character walks upstairs one day and never comes back on the show (I'm talking about you, Judy from *Family Matters*!) and the producers assume that the viewers just won't notice. Oh, we notice!

- **Be thoughtful about the order of the communication.** In some cases, it goes a very long way if you communicate an exit to certain people first before the entire team is told. For example, if a manager is leaving, it may be important to tell the manager's direct reports first, then the rest of the team.

- **Faster is better.** Often, we drag out exits. A team member resigns, and we ask them to stay for three months for a handover. Or we let someone go for performance issues, but we have them work an additional two months as a transition period. Of course, from a financial standpoint, support your team members as is appropriate (through severance or search time), but it's better for the rest of the team, and often for the sanity of the person leaving, for the exit to happen quickly. People grow bitter, things become less productive, and it gets awkward the longer the period between exit decision and actual exit.

- **Use exit interviews to learn.** When possible, conduct exit interviews with employees who leave. You may have specific questions or it may be open-ended, but provide the employees an opportunity to share their feedback or any remaining concerns or comments they have. Use these as an opportunity to learn and grow.

- **And finally, life is (hopefully) long, so focus on positive relationships.** Continue to remind yourself to be kind and empathetic throughout the exiting process. I know this sounds simple, but trust me, it does get hard during some messy exits! Build an informal alumni network with folks who have left your organization. Stay in touch with people you've managed. Check in after people have left the team to see how they are doing. Offer support and guidance where you can.

I once was on a team where one of our favorite team members, Pasha, was a poor performer. He was let go, but the process couldn't have gone any better. We helped him find a new job that was far more aligned with his skills and passions, and every member of the team supported him through the transition. On Pasha's final day, we had a champagne toast where he teared up when describing how loving the exit process had been. On the other hand, I was on another team where a team member, Kirsten, quit by leaving the office when the rest of us were in a meeting. When we walked out of the conference room, she was gone, and her desk was clear except for a note telling us that she was done. I don't blame her. We had managed her performance terribly and did an appalling job helping her fit into the organization.

No matter what, exits are a challenge. You'll spend hours agonizing over the decision of whether you should let an underperformer go. You'll spend hours trying to figure out how to pick up the extra work that a top performer leaves behind when they go. You'll spend hours drafting emails and talking points to communicate an exit to your team. No matter how many hours you spend, some exits will go great and some exits will be a complete and utter disaster. The advice in this chapter will tip the balance: more great exits and fewer disasters. Good luck.

TL;DR

- Managing exits is one of the most challenging and time-consuming activities you'll do as a manager.

- Along with managing the person leaving, you'll spend time and energy managing the team left behind.

- There are three types of exits: when people quit, when they are let go because of performance or other issues, or when people are laid off because of economic or strategic changes in your organization.

- Like most things with being a great manager, communication is key. Communicating to your team the plan for the departure, the timeline, and potentially the reasons behind the exit is particularly important.

A FINAL NOTE ON HIRING AND FIRING

Change is hard on a team. Whether the change comes from a new team member joining an existing team, or a beloved team member leaving, we all struggle with transitions. As a manager, you guide your team through lots of changes, both good and bad.

But what's important to remember is that not all team members will experience the change with the same reactions. The recruitment of a new team member might be incredibly exciting for Taylor, who can now share her workload, but might be incredibly disappointing for Joe, who thought that he would be promoted into the new joiner's role. A strategic pivot for the organization might be very scary for a team member whose best work friend was laid off but invigorating and clarifying for another team member who feels like the organization is better positioned to succeed.

In the good old days (1991), William Bridges, a change consultant, developed a framework that conveys what people experience after a big change occurs.[1] He focuses on the period right after change (the "transition" period) and the different emotions people experience. For example, the CEO of your company leaves. That's the *change*. As a manager at that company, you now need to manage your team members through this *transition* period. According to Bridges, the transition period happens in three stages: endings, exploration, and new beginnings. Each period has a number of feelings associated with it.[2]

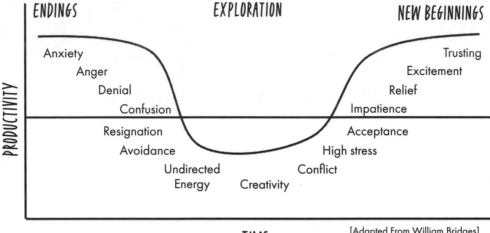

TRANSITIONS AFTER CHANGE

ENDINGS   EXPLORATION   NEW BEGINNINGS

Anxiety   Trusting
  Anger   Excitement
    Denial   Relief
      Confusion   Impatience

Resignation   Acceptance
  Avoidance   High stress
        Undirected   Conflict
        Energy   Creativity

PRODUCTIVITY

TIME   [Adapted From William Bridges]

Unsurprisingly, the period of endings brings about feelings of loss, anger, anxiety, and confusion. This is the period of letting go. The period of exploration is the funky in-between state. The old world order is gone, but the new one isn't yet in place or fully functional. Feelings of uncertainty really take hold during this period. Lastly, the period of new beginnings is just that: Individuals feel excitement as the new world order begins to take shape.

So as a manager, you can help your team members navigate periods of transition—whether it's the transition after a favorite team member leaves, or the transition after a new boss comes on board. The first thing to do is just acknowledge that different members of your team may experience transitions on a different timeline. For example, you might quickly get to the new-beginnings stage after the change happens. Your favorite team member leaves, and you're immediately super excited to let go of the old and start the new because their leaving means tons more opportunity for you. But your team may still be in the period of endings. So you're managing from a place of being all pumped up and enthusiastic about the future, but what your team really needs is space and empathy to process letting go of the past.

What's the best way to manage change? Communicate and communicate some more. Acknowledge the change and the emotions that people may be experiencing. Encourage your team to share what they are feeling with regards to the change. Share this diagram with them so that they can also understand that the team may be in very different places with regards to the change. Talk about what plans are in place as a result of the change.

In whatever way possible, help your team gain agency and control in managing the transition. Perhaps this means that team members help with designing the onboarding for the new senior leader coming on board. Encourage your team to provide feedback and provide solutions for what could have been done better to manage the transition.

And work with your team to continue to get comfortable with uncertainty that is inherent in any organization.[3] Learning how to manage uncertainty is the stuff of Buddhist monks and other enlightened beings, but you can support your team in this quest by encouraging them to be curious (instead of fearful) about uncertainty, continuing to talk through and be open about their concerns, focusing on the areas of their job that they can control, and meditating. Lots and lots of meditating.

TEAM DYNAMICS

Many moons ago, I was part of an absolutely horrible, no good, very bad team. We were a motley crew working on a large project in Kazakhstan, and no matter how hard we tried, we could not get our act together as a team. There was confusion over roles, unclear objectives, and poor project leadership, as well as backstabbing, infighting, and just utter disgust between certain team members. Well, the powers that be thought that expert team builders (former employees of the large consulting firm whose name rhymes with BicMinsey) might be able to salvage our sorry lot with some trust exercises and other activities involving sticky notes and whiteboards. At the end of the first day, I feigned a stomachache and snuck back to my room as the rest of the team was forced to partake in a bonding ritual our khaki-clad team builders called "The Philosopher's Dinner."

The idea behind the Philosopher's Dinner was simple: Every team member was required to bring a meaningful personal item that allowed the rest of the team to learn a little bit more about them. The team builders hoped that when we saw each other as multifaceted, empathic, complex humans, we would end up hating each other less as teammates. And voilà! Our team problems would be solved!

Since I was off playing hooky, I heard about all this from my friend and colleague Rodney. To start the dinner, our project leader went first and shared a piece of organ music, explaining his long love of baroque music. Another team member shared his grandfather's watch and explained the significance of his relationship with him. Next came Victor, our mostly silent colleague who typically spent the day ignoring the rest of us and watching the Kazakh equivalent of YouTube. He took a drawn-out sip of his red wine, slowly reached into his coat, and placed a Makarov pistol on the table.[1] To the silent and shocked team, he said: "I show you this gun to share that though I am quiet, I expect people to take me seriously." Needless to say, the team freaked, and our ex-BicMinsey trainers were on the next flight out of Central Asia. We went back to our passive-aggressive, dysfunctional ways and made sure to always ask Victor if he would like a coffee or pastry or absolutely anything else to make his day better.

I sometimes joke that the optimal team size is zero because being on a bad team is far worse than working alone. Like family, you can't often choose who is on your team. Unlike family, you can't outright scream at obnoxious team members. A bad team takes up way too much time to get way too little work done. A bad team can bring out the most annoying traits in people. And a bad team eats away at your soul.

But teams are often necessary, and great teams are fulfilling, motivating, creative, and hugely productive. We feel immense love toward our teams, show our teams dogged loyalty, and repeatedly go into battle with them. Our great teams have the power to inspire us to be better colleagues and people.

Our great teams have the power to inspire us to be better colleagues and people.

Managing a team is different from managing an individual: There are unique situations and relationships at play within a group. In the next section, we are diving into team dynamics and exploring the funny things that happen when a group of people come together to get work done. We'll discuss the inevitable fights your team will have and talk about ways to make sure that everyone on your team has a voice. And we'll talk about how to right the ship if you find yourself on a team that is quickly sinking.

My hope is that you never have a Kazakhstan-like team situation, despite its endless usefulness as a cocktail party story. And, dear reader, if you follow the tips for managing a great team, I have no doubt that the only reason you'll buy your team members a pastry is because of genuine care and affection for them.

CHAPTER 18

THE TINO (TEAM IN NAME ONLY)

L et's do a little thought experiment. You decide to build a beach house. You design a gorgeous kitchen with a subway tile backsplash and a sleek range hood worthy of the most epic home-decor Instagram influencer. You spend lots of time picking out the perfect white bed linens that somehow always look ironed to match the nautical-themed bedside tables. You design a custom living room chandelier that conveys the perfect balance of rustic charm with subtle Bauhaus sophistication. You imagine guests exclaiming their admiration of the light fixture, and you responding with a throaty, "This ol' thing?" Then a rogue wave comes in from the ocean and destroys your entire house because you spent more time on the mason jar sconces than the house's foundation.

That's how we often approach teams. We spend lots of time curating the "perfect" team, finding the right team members who complement each other, being thoughtful about how we divvy up our team's tasks, and running finely orchestrated meetings. We are then appalled when our team comes crashing down. We are shocked that our perfect team is actually just a flimsy collection of individuals who can't withstand any hardship. Unwittingly, we've created a TINO—a team in name only. That's because a great team, like our beach house, needs a strong foundation built early in the team's life. And like laying cement, the foundation-building of a team is not sexy work: it happens through small, repeated actions that take time and commitment.

**A great team needs a strong foundation
built early in the team's life.**

To manage a great team, you need to deliberately put in place key ingredients from the get-go. And if you are already stuck in the situation of managing a TINO, do not fear: there is still time to turn your team around.

There are countless books, articles, and podcasts that talk about what makes a high-functioning team. In my work and studies, I've found that the most practical and effective research comes from a study conducted by Google a number of years ago called Project Aristotle. Google's work is unique in its simplicity and scale. Essentially, Google ran a study examining 180 teams across its organization.[1] Google found that its high-functioning teams weren't necessarily similar on structural attributes like diversity (e.g., some high-functioning teams were comprised of a mix of ages and backgrounds, others were homogenous) and didn't all use the same operating norms (e.g., some high-functioning teams were viciously efficient with time, others were laxer and looser with timekeeping). Rather, all of the high-functioning teams shared the same two ingredients: a strong foundation of norms and psychological safety.

The Ingredients for the Optimal Team

1. Explicit norms

2. Psychological safety

> For teams to be successful, it doesn't matter what
> the norms are; rather, it matters that everyone on
> the team operates from the same set of norms.

Let's discuss both in turn and then talk about how you incorporate these ingredients into your team.

1. **Explicit Norms:** Norms are the ways we operate, the "rules of the game." Interestingly, for teams to be successful, it doesn't matter what the norms are; rather, it matters that everyone on the team operates from the same set of norms. For example, a team that spends the first twenty minutes of the weekly check-in meeting talking about their Saturday night escapades and then slowly meanders into an agendaless meeting can be just as successful as a team that jumps right to business and sticks to a relevant-info-only, tightly managed conversation. What matters is that everyone on the team knows what to expect and operates from the same playbook.

2. **Psychological Safety:** The concept of psychological safety, first developed by psychologist Amy Edmondson, means that individuals on a team are safe to take risks without fear of retribution or humiliation.2 Teams that have high levels of psychological safety allow each team member to contribute fully. Psychological safety is comprised of two components:
   - **Empathy:** Team members know where others are "coming from" and work to understand the perspective and experience of others in the group.[3]
   - **Conversational turn taking:** Each team member has a voice, and there is an overall balance of team members speaking up ("overall" meaning over the life of the team—it does not mean that for every meeting each team member has to speak an equal amount of time).

If you want to know how much psychological safety your team has (and track your progress toward more psychological safety), Edmondson and her team share the survey that tests it. You can find the psychological safety survey in the appendix.

So these are the ingredients that you need to build into your team: explicit norms, lots of empathy, and conversational turn taking.[4] Now, here's *how* you can start building them into your team as a manager.

EXPLICIT NORMS

At the beginning of team formation, sit down with your team and write down your team norms. Like many things in life, often we have an implicit set of expectations in our head that have never been made explicit. Make your thinking visible and write down the expectations for your team.

Answer tactical questions like "What is our preferred mode of communication?" and more value-driven questions like "Do we value efficiency or effectiveness more?"

Talk through how decisions are made (e.g., unanimous, majority rules, team leader has final say) and assign team roles. Again, it's less important what the norm is (unanimous isn't inherently better than majority voting); it's more important that everyone knows what the norm is.

Revisit your team norms frequently. Sometimes, you may have to adapt norms as the situation at work changes (e.g., you move from in-person to virtual work) or because new members have joined the team.

There's a template in the appendix to help facilitate this discussion with your team.

EMPATHY

Some folks naturally have more empathy than others. That's okay. What you can do with your team is build the empathy muscle, which is helping team members understand each other's perspectives. Best case—people are open and vulnerable with their team members and empathy is built. Team members talk about who they are and what's important to them. But this is hard, especially if the team is new or the team is already suffering from some issues.

So, instead, I like to use a tool like StrengthsFinder or the Enneagram that highlights individuals' different working styles.[5] I don't necessarily subscribe to the blunt categorization of people that inevitably results from these types of surveys; however, I do like how these tools help folks talk about themselves in the context of their different strengths (and often this leads to an open conversation about individuals' weaknesses). Again, the tool is a means to an end: the goal is to get people talking about themselves in an open way that allows others to better understand who they are and where they are coming from.

You could kick off a monthly or bimonthly meeting with a beautiful question aimed to build empathy and understanding of team members.

Encourage team members to share more about their personal lives in a way that lets the rest of the team understand their backgrounds, what

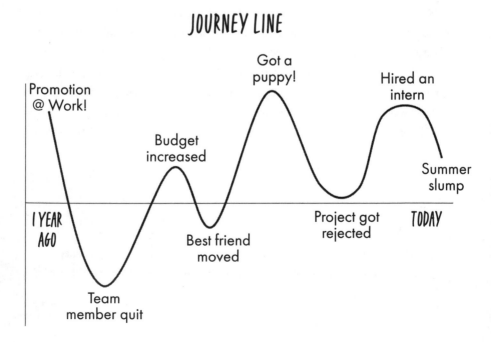

JOURNEY LINE

might be challenging to them in a non-work context, or why they might be responding to a question or discussion in a particular way. To do so, I like using a tool called "Journey Lines"—like the previous page—to facilitate conversation with your team. Each person on your team maps out their year—their highs and lows—and then discusses it with the group. It's a great way for your team to get to know each other better.

Another way to build empathy on your team? Trust falls! (Just kidding.)

CONVERSATIONAL TURN TAKING

This means that everyone on the team has a voice and isn't oppressed by the group or a member of the group. In the next chapter, we will spend lots of time talking about how to make your team feel comfortable and welcome speaking up. But as a special sneak preview, here are a few ways to build conversational turn taking on your team:

Appoint a devil's advocate for important decisions. It will help your team build the muscle of dissenting and help your team members get more comfortable opposing the views of the group.

Create a norm where the most junior member of the team speaks first in team meetings.

Encourage your team members to ask each other questions—not just ask questions to you, the manager.

"Warm call" members of your team during discussions to ensure voices are heard. Warm calling, when you direct a question in a group to a particular person, is particularly helpful during virtual meetings when it's hard to read body language and other cues that might create openings for people to speak up. (For example, "Leslie, what did you think of the second recommendation coming out of the pitch presentation?")

For those team members who are total air hogs, give them constructive feedback about the balance of time they spend speaking during team meetings versus listening. And feel comfortable interrupting them if they are speaking too much (and letting them know in advance that you will most definitely do this!).

I've been part of so many TINOs in my career that I've lost count. These TINOs ranged from grad-school teams (nothing is more passive-aggressive than five graduate students attempting to finish a group paper) to executive teams (gotta love a group of execs who truly loathe each other attempting to run a start-up together), to consulting teams (I was on one that was so bad that three of the eight team members all quit within three weeks of each other). And most recently, I was part of a team at a yoga retreat. I thought for sure that a bunch of self-actualized yogis would make a fantastic set of team members—wrong. We faced the same misaligned expectations, letdowns, and disappointments that any corporate TINO experiences (but just in a tropical setting). But there's hope. Make your norms explicit and build psychological safety on your team. And trust falls. Lots of trust falls.

TL;DR

- Sometimes, our team stinks. A TINO is a team in name only—a group of individuals who should function as a team but instead function like a bunch of sole operators.

- To build and manage a great team, you need two primary components: explicit norms and psychological safety (which is driven by empathy and conversational turn taking).

- It doesn't matter what your team norms are, as long as everyone on the team is aware of the norms and subscribes to them.

- Empathy on a team is driven by team members understanding where others are coming from; using an activity like Journey Lines is an easy way to start that process.

- Conversational turn taking means each team member has a voice and, over time, spends about the same time talking in meetings. Appoint a devil's advocate and be comfortable shushing the overtalker in your team meetings.

CHAPTER 19

GETTING YOUR TEAM TO SPEAK UP

Way back when, on a steaming hot summer day, a family somewhere in the middle of Texas was sitting on their porch, sweating bullets, with absolutely nothing to do. Grandpa throws out a few ideas to beat the heat and get a change of scenery, none of which seem too appealing. Grandma suggests a couple more ideas, including jumping in the car and driving the whole family, including the dog, to Abilene, another steaming hot city with not much going on.

Mom asks Dad, "Do you want to go to Abilene?"

Dad says, "Meh."

Junior asks Grandpa, "Do you want to go to Abilene?" To which he responds with a noncommittal shrug, and so it goes. Junior, Mom, Dad, Baby Texan, Grandpa, Grandma, *and* the dog all recognize that going to Abilene is a terrible idea and no one actually wants to go. But lo and behold, they somehow find themselves driving in their un-air-conditioned Dodge Caravan to Abilene, which was, in fact, a far worse outcome than just sitting on the porch at home.

Thus, the Abilene paradox was born—the situation when a group of people collectively decide on a course of action that is counter to the actual preferences of many (or all) of the individuals in the group.

We've all seen the Abilene paradox happen before. Think about the last time you were with a group of friends trying to decide on a place to eat . . . and somehow you ended up at the mediocre restaurant down the street that no one really likes. Now think about when the Abilene paradox has reared its ugly head at work. Someone throws out an idea (often the first that comes to mind), and because no one wants to offer a healthy challenge, we end up going with it despite no one actually thinking the idea is great. Or how about when we hire the candidate who is everyone's third or fourth choice—often someone who doesn't have any strong negative qualities but also doesn't really have any strong positive ones either. Folks come out of the hiring meeting scratching their heads, thinking, "How the heck did we just end up hiring that dude?"

As a manager, you are in charge of leading teams to efficient and effective decisions. The hard thing about managing teams is that when we get a group of people together, that group falls prey to funky situations like the Abilene paradox and other forms of groupthink. Bad decisions are made because no one spoke out (or the team did not listen when someone did). To manage your team well, you need to make sure that your team feels comfortable and excited about speaking up (sharing their opinions and ideas) and speaking out (disagreeing and dissenting with others' opinions, especially yours). And you need to make sure that when members of the team do speak up and out, their voices are truly heard despite their level of seniority or standing in the organization.

Let's first briefly touch on *why* it is important to make sure your team can speak up and speak out. Our teams make worse decisions when we don't consider opposing viewpoints or all the potential information at hand. History books are littered with examples of high-profile teams making catastrophic decisions because they let groupthink and the Abilene paradox get the better of them. This is how the space shuttle *Challenger* crashed despite scientific evidence that could have prevented the disaster, and why the blood diagnostic company Theranos was able to deceitfully operate without an actual product despite being overseen by a board of brilliant and respected individuals.[1] It's also why a thoughtful individual at Uber finds himself pushing forward a questionable and unethical strategy aimed at deceiving government officials.[2]

> **To be a great manager, make sure your team feels comfortable speaking up and speaking out.**

Another reason why it's important to ensure your team can speak up and out is because it creates an inclusive, anti-oppressive team culture. Specifically, it's important that you don't lean on a sense of urgency or efficiency as a justification for not including your team members' voices. A sense of urgency—and using it as a reason to not be inclusive of others' opinions—is one way that people in power (often inadvertently or subconsciously) perpetuate the status quo of privilege.[3]

It's easy for us to think *My team would never make such horrible decisions* and *My team always has healthy debate and tells me the truth*. But often the forces of groupthink happen in a Jedi-like way: not only do we not see them coming, but also we don't know when they've even happened.

Let's now talk about *why* it's hard for our teams to speak up and out and *why* groupthink happens without us even knowing that it's occurring (our subconscious is at play again!).

WHY WE DO LIKE GWEN AND DON'T SPEAK

DEEP DOWN WE ALL WANT TO BE PART OF THE POPULAR CROWD

It's hard for an individual to have a differing opinion from the rest of a group because it creates severe anxiety when one's opinion is in the minority. Psychologist Solomon Asch conducted a famous experiment that showed that individuals would rather be wrong than propose an opposing opinion to a group.[4] And that the experience of knowing that the group is wrong creates immense stress on the system. We care about what people think of us, so we conform to a group's ideas even if we know those ideas are wrong.

INFORMATION, LIKE A GREAT TIKTOK, IS BETTER WHEN SHARED (OR IS IT?)

In groups, we end up talking about shared information that we all already know. I like to call this the high school friends' phenomenon. You know, what happens when you're with your friends from high school and you spend your time talking about shared memories and common friends, as opposed to talking about anything new going on. In a group, it's hard to bring up new information despite that info being helpful or critical. And what's crazy is that experts suffer this same fate. Research shows that physicians in a group fell into the trap of talking about shared information as opposed to unique information when diagnosing a patient, resulting in the wrong clinical diagnosis.[5]

OUR BRAINS ARE EASILY CONTAMINATED

We are influenced by others' judgments even if we don't realize it. This is a process called *mental contamination*, and it prevents us from sharing our unbiased opinions. Think about a brainstorming session where we all happen to circle around the first idea that was brought up or the idea that was brought up by the most senior member of the team. It's because we've been mentally contaminated.

WE LET OUR WHITE FLAGS FLY

When we're in a group, we often do something called "raising the white flag."[6] It's when a team member mentally checks out of a discussion and stops caring about the decision at hand. It's the point in the conversation when team member Jacques starts thinking about lunch and whether poké is actually healthy; or when teammate Stevie is so sick of sitting in a sweaty conference room that he'll agree with any decision as long as it gets him out of the meeting. We end up raising the white flag when we feel like other people have more expertise than us, or when we feel like the decision doesn't directly impact us, or when we lack the confidence that we can contribute meaningfully.

NO ONE LIKES CANTANKEROUS CARRIE

And for a final reason why it's challenging to speak out (and perhaps the reason most important to remember when managing younger team members) is that we all want to be liked. And who do we like? We like people who are agreeable and validating of our brilliant ideas. So a junior person in a team is going to want to come across as likable, which means they are

WHAT YOUR TEAM IS SAYING

WHAT YOUR TEAM IS THINKING

not going to pooh-pooh an idea, especially an idea put forward by their brilliant manager (you).

Okay, we now know why. So the next question is how: How do you as a manager encourage your team to speak up and speak out?

WAYS TO GET YOUR TEAM TALKING

- **Solicit differing opinions and ideas.** Sometimes, all people need is an invitation to dance. Make it a part of your management practice to always ask for people's opinions and truly listen when they give them.

- **Appoint a devil's advocate.** Have a big decision you're trying to make with your team? Nominate one person in your group who is responsible for bringing up the opposite point of view for each of the arguments. Not only will it help result in a better-informed and stronger decision, but also it will help junior people build the muscle of disagreeing. Similarly, don't just ask your team *en masse*: "Does everyone agree?" and let people nod their heads. Instead ask each person in turn: "Ashley, do you agree?" and "Erin, can you point out one reason why this decision won't work?"

- **Brainstorm—but brainstorm alone.** If you're planning a meeting where you want to brainstorm a whole bunch of ideas, have your team members come up with ideas independently before the meeting. The group's ideas will be more creative and diverse because they will suffer less from mental contamination. The same goes for building arguments for a decision—have folks write down before the meeting their arguments or facts to inform a group decision.

- **Praise and reward dissent.** Build a culture on your team where bravery in speaking out is praised openly and rewarded (e.g., promotions, more responsibility, employee recognition). Some organizations have "dissent" as one of their cultural pillars and state that every employee has an *obligation* to dissent.

> **Build a culture on your team where bravery in speaking out is praised openly and rewarded.**

- **Speak last as the manager.** Folks hate to hear this, but once you get a little bit of power, people treat you differently. Despite the fact that you're cool, hip, and fun to be around, your team may still exhibit deferential behavior toward you and change their opinions based on yours. So speak last and ask the most junior members of your team to offer their opinions first.

- **Name it.** Let your team know what "raising the white flag" is, and then call them out when they do it. When someone starts to check out, simply say, "Hey, Miyuki, you're raising the white flag. What's going through your mind?" Trust me: it's much easier to use a neutral phrase than say, "Hey Miyuki, stop being a stinky teammate who is obviously annoyed by this conversation."

I would be remiss if I didn't alert you, dear reader, that for some individuals, speaking up and speaking out might be particularly challenging or complicated. And the end goal you seek as a manager is for voices and dissenting opinions to be heard and considered, in whatever shape that takes. For example, a Black male student of mine shared how he limits how much he speaks up and speaks out so as not to be seen as overly aggressive or confrontational. I've been in situations before as the only woman on a team and have limited what I say and what I disagree with (sometimes consciously, sometimes unconsciously).

Perhaps this point was made most poignant to me at one of my prior start-ups. We had a team meeting where we spent a good chunk of time discussing the importance of junior team members speaking up—and that it was a huge part of our organization's culture. A woman on our team, Claire, who is from China, raised her hand. After telling her that she didn't have to raise her hand in team meetings, we asked her what she wanted to share. Claire told us that, the way she was raised in China, the value that was drilled into her day in and day out was to think about her thought *three times* before verbally sharing it. So our push for her to immediately speak up when an idea popped into her head was diametrically opposed to her cultural values. We then rethought the message we were sending to our team and rethought how to ensure Claire's—and others'—ideas were heard. For example, we started pausing more after asking a question to allow introverts to gather their thoughts before sharing, and we encouraged written commentary before and after discussions to allow for an alternative to a fast-moving debate where the loudest and quickest voices often dominated.

If you're a new manager, you may feel insecure and vulnerable that your team doesn't think you are smart, competent, or worthy of our role. Even seasoned managers sometimes feel this way. The risk is that your insecurity may manifest itself in talking way too much in meetings, in order to appear as if you know the answer to all questions, and not allowing your ideas or decisions to be exposed to weaknesses or debate. You may be particularly sensitive to a team member disagreeing with a decision you are not confident in. But push against that insecurity and those behaviors. It's much better to get your team to speak up and speak out—you'll ultimately be far more competent as a manager if you do so. And your team will build their voice and abilities, there will be better decisions and outcomes, and it's much more fun to be part of a team where ideas are flowing, folks feel safe disagreeing, and no one gets stuck going to Abilene.

TL;DR

- The Abilene Paradox and groupthink, more generally, are powerful phenomena that impact teams. If we aren't careful, our teams may make bad decisions that no one is happy with.

- These phenomena often happen because people want to be liked and be seen in a positive light by those around them, especially by those who are more senior than they are.

- We also have the tendency to "raise the white flag" in a group—we mentally check out of group discussions and stop offering our ideas.

- It falls on you, as a manager, to create a set of behaviors, norms, and a culture that encourages your team to speak up and speak out.

- So nominate a devil's advocate, brainstorm alone, reward dissent, and speak last as a manager.

- And make sure your strategies account for different cultural, racial, and gender dynamics, as these also come into play in a group.

CHAPTER 20

THE GOOD FIGHT: CONFLICT AND WHAT TO DO ABOUT IT

One early evening, I was on a power walk with a friend, Vy. Typical of these walks, we were discussing work. Vy started bemoaning the fact that her team was plagued by conflict. As we pumped our arms and swung our hips, Vy proceeded to tell me about the fights, disagreements, and shouting matches her team was having. Right before she started to ponder what strategies she could use to improve the conflict on the team, I cheekily asked her: "Well, what type of conflict is your team having? What are you guys fighting about?"

Despite its negative connotation, conflict is not inherently bad or good. At times, conflict is awful—we fight over intractable differences and fight because we fundamentally don't agree with the beliefs of our teammates (or family members or life partners). We feel resentment and anger toward those that are conflictual toward us. Projects and teams (and marriages) are derailed over this type of conflict. But fighting can be good, and fighting well is a necessary skill (as long exalted by couple's therapists everywhere). Productive conflict reduces groupthink and tests our implicit and potentially biased assumptions. Conflict generates new and innovative ideas.

Conflict is not inherently bad or good. Fighting can be good, and fighting well is a necessary skill.

On many teams, all conflict feels the same. We're shouting at each other; people feel disrespected and get huffy. A disagreement about when to meet snowballs into simmering ire about how one teammate is just *so* selfish. But there are distinct types of conflict and understanding what we're fighting about is critical: we can then understand if our conflict is productive or damaging. To be a great manager, it's important to know what types of conflict your team is experiencing and what to do about it.[1]

THE THREE TYPES OF CONFLICT AND WHAT DRIVES THEM

RELATIONSHIP CONFLICT

Ah, this is the conflict that's really stinky. This is the conflict that results because of entrenched differences among team members around beliefs, values, and interpersonal incompatibilities. In short, this is the type of conflict that happens when you really just don't like your team member and fundamentally disagree with how they view the world.

Relationship conflict destroys teams. It's unproductive, annihilates trust, and ruins communication. High-performing teams have low levels of relationship conflict throughout their lives.

So what do you do as a manager? Go back to the fundamentals of building a great team that we discussed in chapter 18: focus on trust building, empathy, and getting your team to know each other in a deeper way.

Psychologist Lori Gottlieb writes, "It's impossible to get to know people deeply and not come to like them."[2] For really bad bouts of relationship conflict, you need to get your team to a place where they deeply know each other and build a sense of liking.

One challenge with relationship conflict is that it's often between two members on a team, but the negativity spills over into the rest of the team (yup—that's right, astute reader. It's another form of emotional contagion). So as a manager, you may need to work through these bilateral frictions to support the rest of the team's functioning.

TASK CONFLICT

Yay to task conflict! Task conflict is the result of disagreements about ideas or the actual work getting done. For example, if your team is in a heated debate about whether your new product should contain a bell or a whistle; or whether candidate A or candidate B is better for the role you're hiring—that's task conflict.

Task conflict helps teams perform better! As we discussed in the last chapter, disagreements can reduce groupthink and test implicit biases. Task conflict generates new and innovative ideas. Strong teams have a healthy amount of task conflict. You should be concerned if your team never disagrees about anything.

So what do you do as a manager? First and foremost, make sure your team is not homogeneous. Differences in backgrounds, experiences, functions, ages, etc., can all help with task conflict. We each bring our different perspectives and lived experiences to a problem at hand.

The other ways to encourage task conflict are very similar to the ways of discouraging groupthink: Appoint a devil's advocate; brainstorm, but brainstorm alone; encourage and reward healthy debate; and reward and praise individuals on your team who are great at dissenting.

PROCESS CONFLICT

Ah, the goldilocks of conflict. Process conflict is the disagreements the team gets in about scheduling, logistics, assigning work, and the overall process of how work gets done. Process conflict often occurs at the beginning and end of projects, as tasks are getting allocated, and as a project is about to be completed.

Process conflict is necessary, but too much can frustrate team members and lead to (*gasp*) relationship conflict. Personally, process conflict drives me bananas. I hate spending time disagreeing over schedules or about who does what. But this conflict helps with figuring out the most effective way of getting work done. Furthermore, when there isn't healthy debate over process, team members can get resentful over work allocation or deadlines.

So what do you do as a manager? It's all about going back to the fundamentals of a strong team. Establish clear norms about how work typically gets done, how the team approaches big decisions (for example, consensus versus majority versus leader-driven decisions), and how meetings typically run. The more your team sticks to these norms and develops a routine around how work gets done, the more effective your process conflict becomes.

Specifically, figure out how to resolve process conflict when it happens. For example, when your team disagrees on meeting times, how is that disagreement resolved? Teams that have process conflict but then resolve it quickly are high-performing.

Simple things like always having your meetings on a Wednesday, or using the same Zoom number for every team call, or having a rotating note taker for meetings removes some of the frictions that might result in unnecessary process conflict.

So what do these three types of conflict look like on a high-performing team?[3] Relationship conflict is low throughout, task conflict spikes in the middle, and process conflict is higher at the beginning and the end of a project.

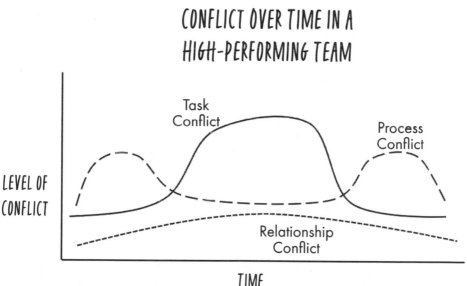

CONFLICT OVER TIME IN A HIGH-PERFORMING TEAM

Task Conflict

Process Conflict

LEVEL OF CONFLICT

Relationship Conflict

TIME

One team I was part of was exceptionally rife with conflict. Our business was struggling and we fought about how to right the ship. The tactics deployed in our fights included (but were not limited to) drowning out others' ideas by yelling loudly; the silent treatment; spontaneous bursts of crying; strategic bursts of crying; apathy; and outright denial that there was conflict. Our conflict over our ideas about how to fix the business (task conflict) and how to make the decision about which idea to go with (process conflict) quickly escalated into relationship conflict. And once it got to relationship conflict, trust got destroyed, and it was hard to recover.

I share this to illustrate that I know conflict is messy and that simply putting conflict in three neat categories is not a quick, easy fix. But being more mindful about the type of conflict your team is experiencing and making your team aware of when that conflict is good helps to prevent the negative spiral that can result. So next time you're yelling at a teammate or quietly seething but afraid to bring an opposing viewpoint to your group, think about what you're fighting for.

Conflict is messy. But prevent it from spiraling by making your team aware of when the conflict might be good.

Happy fighting!

TL;DR

- Conflict is neither good nor bad. Some types of conflict are productive, while others are detrimental to team functioning.

- Relationship conflict results from interpersonal incompatibilities. Relationship conflict hurts team trust, communication, and ultimately team functioning.

- Task conflict results from disagreements about work product or ideas. Teams, especially those focused on creative tasks, should embrace and encourage task conflict.

- Process conflict is the disagreements that result from logistics, scheduling, and planning how work gets done. Process conflict is often a necessary part of every team, but process conflict that gets out of hand can ultimately hurt your team.

CHAPTER 21

THE MEETING PARADOX: WE HATE GOING, BUT WE STILL WANT TO BE INVITED

L et's begin with a story. Precious joined a start-up as the CEO's executive assistant. She wasn't totally psyched that her first job out of college involved a lot of scheduling, managing travel logistics, and occasionally taking lunch orders, but what she did love was taking notes. Long, tedious notes. Why, you might ask, did Precious love taking notes so much? Well, it was because Precious, in her role, got to join all of the CEO's meetings to make sure meeting notes were captured. Precious got to be in the meeting when the CEO closed the start-up's first huge deal, the deal that allowed the company to continue operating. She was in the meeting when the leadership team decided to restructure the company. Precious was in the room when the Series B was finalized.

There's power in being in the room where it happens. As a junior person, you soak in so much when you're surrounded by people with more experience than you. Being a fly on the wall when senior people are making large strategic decisions, or clients are talking about their product challenges, or a vendor is doing some hardcore negotiating with your boss, is so rewarding. You learn and grow by witnessing these situations and being included in meetings.

But let's look at the other side. Recently, I had an epic text conversation with a friend about discontinued Trader Joe's items. It was incredibly involved, detailed, and extensive as she fervently took screenshots of Reddit posts and added her own commentary to the conspiracy theories about why some products vanished from the TJ's shelves. What was she doing during our text exchange? Sitting in a meeting at work. Here's another one: I was on a thirty-person Zoom call. It was highly productive . . . in that I bought clearance athleisurewear, found a new dentist, checked the current price of Bitcoin, and submitted a few applications on puppy adoption sites. And I'm sure—in the last week, no less—you have had that feeling in a meeting where you pause and silently ask yourself: "Why exactly am I here again?"

Meetings. Are. The. Worst.

We are fatigued by meetings. As an organization scales, coordination becomes more difficult, and often the most-used solution to address our coordination problem is more meetings: update meetings, cross-functional meetings, brainstorming meetings, weekly stand-ups, and mandatory "fun" meetings. It gets to a point where decisions can't be made without a meeting. We don't want to upset anyone, so we invite everyone to join the meeting—just in case.

Herein lies the paradox: As a manager, you want to involve all of your team members in meetings. You want to support your team members' development, and meetings are a great opportunity for growth. And you want to be sensitive to the common complaint that when a start-up gets bigger, people (especially early joiners) feel more and more disconnected from decision-making. Yet excessive meetings with too many participants are unproductive and frankly just not a good use of time. Your team can become crippled under the weight of worthless meetings.

So what do you do? To be a great manager, you need to treat your approach to meetings (and who you invite) with as much care, diligence, and thought as you would treat a work product, an investor pitch, a new hire, or a sales call.

Treat your meeting strategy with as much care as you would treat an investor pitch or an important sales call.

I've talked about how to help your team make effective decisions, and I've talked about the norms and expectations you can set with your team. Both of these will improve the success of your meetings. And there are additional ways you can productively manage your team meetings and still make sure that your team members continue to feel included and continue to benefit from the exposure that meetings provide.

WAYS TO SAVE YOUR SANITY AND RUN EFFECTIVE TEAM MEETINGS

1. Embrace the meeting paradox.
   - Tell your team that not everyone can and is going to get invited to every meeting. Encourage your team to discuss their concerns. Acknowledge that cutting back on meeting attendance is one of the changes that can hurt the most when an organization gets bigger.
   - Work with your teams on their individual development plans and create space for your team members to attend *select* meetings that directly support their growth goals. For example, a team member might want to build long-term sales capabilities; perhaps they sit in on a monthly sales meeting to gain experience in this area.

2. Treat the meeting invite list like the bouncer at the hippest club in town.
   - Be thoughtful about the invite list for every meeting. If an individual does not have a specific role or purpose to be in the meeting, kick them out (that is, don't invite them in the first place).
   - For those team members who are not invited and are likely bummed because they are not, let them know why and make

sure to provide an update after the meeting about what was discussed. They may not be in the room where it happens, but at least, they'll gain insight.

3. Be that person who insists: "No agenda, no meeting."
   - Set an agenda and share it in advance.
   - Include the objective of the meeting (are we making a decision, brainstorming ideas, doing a check-in).
   - Include what is required of the attendees (preread, prework).

4. Embrace your inner theater geek and assign people roles.
   - Do you think it's obvious that the junior person in the room should take notes during a meeting? And then when they don't, do you shoot them passive-aggressive glances?
   - Be crystal clear about everyone's roles during a meeting (that means saying it aloud!).

5. No matter how good you think you are at it, do not multitask during a meeting (and don't allow others to).
   - If you find yourself multitasking during a meeting, ask yourself if you really need to be there. If not, don't attend in the future.
   - Once the boss or most senior person in the meeting starts to multitask, it provides a signal that everyone else can also half check out of the meeting.
   - I mean it. Don't respond to emails. Don't check Instagram. Don't text your mom.

Do not multitask during a meeting . . . Don't respond to emails. Don't check Instagram. Don't text your mom.

6. Be chivalrous: plan the second date while still on the first one.
   - Be clear about follow-up before you end the meeting—*who* is going to do *what* and by *when*?
   - Make sure people are clear about what they are expected to do coming out of the meeting.

- For those folks who weren't in the meeting, send a timely update email about the proceedings. It will be so appreciated!

Virtual meetings suffer from many of the same trials and tribulations as in-person meetings, but often our bad habits or laziness around meeting principles become exacerbated in a virtual format. When running team meetings where people are remote, remember the following:

- Just because it's easy to invite everyone to the meeting when it's on Zoom, it doesn't mean you should. Stick to the same strict guest list principle you have for in-person meetings. In fact, you may even want to be *stricter* with virtual meetings to counteract the multitasking that is easier to do when we're online.

- When leading a virtual meeting, engage with people directly by name, essentially "warm calling" them throughout the meeting. Don't just ask to the grid of faces: "Does anyone have any feedback?" Rather, try: "Soren, what is your reaction to slide 10?" or "Hallie, what is one thing you would change about this decision?"

- Do. Not. Multitask.

- Tell the team to stop being polite. It's super annoying in virtual meetings when half the meeting time is spent with people apologizing for jumping in at the same time or accidentally talking over someone because of a technology lag: "You go ahead." "No, go for it." "That's okay, you go." Then everyone talks at once. Everyone apologizes. Repeat vicious cycle. Ask the team to cut out the apologizing, just talk, and if it's clear that someone isn't getting enough airtime, make sure you, as the team leader, bring that person into the discussion or call on them directly.[1]

- Some organizations effectively use what I like to call the "least common denominator" method of meetings. It means that if one person is on Zoom and the rest of the team is in person, everyone on the team logs into a Zoom account and takes the meeting from their own laptop. Or if one person is on the phone and others are using video, everyone uses the phone. If you're ever been the lone person on Zoom when everyone else is sitting at a conference table chatting away, you'll understand why the least common denominator method helps in ensuring voices are heard and no one is inadvertently excluded from the conversation.

- Along with the least common denominator method of meetings, there's also the I-am-so-sick-of-being-on-video method. Sometimes, it's okay to just have your virtual meeting as a phone call. We get burned out from being on camera all day, and your team may need a break from staring at their screens. Give your team permission to suggest that a virtual meeting is *not* on video.

Every so often, I do a quick meeting audit. I look at all of my standing meetings over the course of a month and take a cold, hard look at their purpose. I get rid of meetings whose objectives could be accomplished through a quick email. I disinvite people to meetings where attendance isn't necessary. I shorten or lengthen meetings to align with the actual objective of what I'm trying to accomplish. Think of it as spring cleaning for your meetings. Or better yet, as the Marie Kondo method for meetings. If the meeting doesn't spark joy, throw it out.

TL;DR

- It's really powerful to be in the room where it happens (i.e., to witness and participate in decisions and strategies that impact your organization).

- Yet as an organization grows, we often find ourselves in way too many meetings, and our meetings are poorly run.

- As a manager, you have a crucial role in ensuring that your team members participate in meetings while also ensuring that meetings are not a waste of time.

- Ways to make your meetings more effective include always setting an agenda, never multitasking, and uninviting people if necessary.

- Be even more careful with virtual meetings to make sure they are productive and useful to all participants.

A FINAL NOTE ON TEAM DYNAMICS

We've talked about how to recruit the right team members, how to manage their transitions, and how to put in place the foundation for a solid team. We've talked about the importance of voice and representation on your team, how emotions can affect your team, and how to approach conflict when it occurs among team members. I have one final cherry to put on the top of the team sundae we've been building in the prior chapters: to build a great team, build a great community.

Ownership. Empathy. Get it done mentality. Curiosity. Efficiency. Customer-centric. Stewardship. Integrity. Passion. Collaboration. Kindness. Move fast. Accountability. Blah blah blah. Courage. Teamwork. Honesty. Respect. Humility.

Often in start-ups, we spend a lot of time talking about our organization's culture. We develop a list of cultural values and post them around the office. We hold workshops solely focused on building culture. We interview candidates based on a list of cultural questions. And we tell everyone that culture is our competitive advantage. But in the daily management of our teams, culture can easily feel like empty words. Our team members struggle to see how they can individually impact the organization's culture or how a cultural value actually maps to their day-to-day work. As our organizations get bigger, our teams may feel like they have a different culture from teams in other parts of the organization. Our cultural values, those words that we were so thoughtful about, all of a sudden start to feel like Halo Top ice cream—slightly unsatisfying, but we can't *quite* put our finger on why.

Culture is important because it implicitly and explicitly tells us how to act in our organizations. Yet when you are managing a team, the broad brush strokes of culture may seem far less relevant. My final thought for you on managing a great team is don't focus on building a great culture. Instead, focus on building a great community.

> **Don't focus on building a great culture. Instead, focus on building a great community.**

I know. I know. This advice seems to contradict oodles of what has been preached about culture.[1] And I'm not saying that culture should be forgotten; rather, I'm saying that focusing on building a strong community on your team, one that is inclusive and participatory, is a far more powerful and useful lens as a manager.

A community is a living, breathing thing that every single person on the team is part of and responsible for nurturing. A true community means no one is excluded and that everyone has a place. A community brings people together around a shared vision or a shared purpose. Everyone has a voice in a community.

> **A true community means no one is excluded and everyone has a place**

Think about the best communities you've ever been a part of. Perhaps it was a college sports team, a church, a beer softball league, a neighborhood, or an alumni group. When you're part of a great community, you feel a strong sense of belonging, you care deeply about the other members of the community, and you also have a set of clear community values. You give back to your community and focus on ways to make the community grow. You relish being part of it, not just understanding or abiding by it. Culture makes you act. Community makes you feel.

How do you build community on your team?

1. **Try replacing "culture" with "community"** in discussions about values, processes, behaviors, and structure. For example, consider the following:
   - What do we want our community to look like?
   - What do we value about our community?
   - What are the activities, behaviors, or processes that can help the community thrive?

   A great example of this in action is how onboarding happens. As we discussed in chapter 16, a consistent, structured onboarding process is critical to the success of a new joiner. But you don't onboard someone into a community, you *welcome* them. So what can you add to your onboarding process to actually make it a welcoming process? (Hint: You still have all of the steps, but you approach it very differently.)

2. **Actively and immediately involve your team in the creation of community.** Community is owned by every single member of the group. Ask your team how they think they can strengthen community. Empower them to make changes that build up their community.

3. And lastly, when implementing internal initiatives, processes, or activities, ask yourself: **How does this serve our community?** Will this initiative strengthen or weaken our community?

As humans, we long for connection but often have few avenues to feel part of something bigger than ourselves. For many of us, the closest we have to true community are our workplaces.[2] Often, we hear people say that they stay at an organization because they love the culture. But what we really love are the people who surround us—our community. We leave organizations when we don't feel connected to a community. So to be a great manager of a team, focus on building not just culture but community!

PART III

MANAGING YOURSELF

MANAGING YOURSELF

Many moons ago, I had a lovely woman, Xinyu, on my team. Xinyu was fresh out of college, working at her first job. One afternoon, Xinyu and I were walking for coffee and ran into a friend of hers. Xinyu introduced me as her "boss." I did a double take, looked around, and then thought, *Oh, shoot, that's right. I'm someone's boss.*

For whatever reason, Xinyu's introduction that afternoon struck me. Perhaps it was her use of the term *boss*, or the realization that Xinyu thought of me not as a peer who sometimes manages her but as this totally separate and formal-sounding entity. She saw me as a boss. I didn't yet see myself as one. My brain didn't know how to make sense of this dissonant information.

I once had a boss talk about her transition from team member to manager as going from "getting things done" to "making sure things get done." She talked about the point at which she realized her role was completely different from what it had been at the start of her career. There's beauty in the simplicity of that statement. As you become a manager, there is a fundamental shift in how you approach your work. And there is a fundamental shift in how others think of you. Yet the move to management is not that simple, partially because you might not think of yourself as yet having made that shift.

> When you become a manager, there is a fundamental shift in how you approach your work, and there is a fundamental shift in how others think of you.

As a manager, you will be faced with the feeling that everyone around you dislikes you (or even worse—loathes you). You will have to confront making a decision or taking a course of action that multiple team members disagree with. There will be times when you feel very alone and separate from your team in a way you hadn't felt before. There will be other times when you will feel awkward and experience lots and lots of discomfort.

You will make mistakes as a manager—and these mistakes will have far bigger consequences than the mistakes you have made in the past. You will hire the wrong person, you will say the wrong thing, you will mismanage a project, you will micromanage, and you will handle an employee exit poorly. You will feel like an impostor and wonder if you are cut out for this role. And you will fear that your team members will realize that you're *not* cut out for this role, and that all of your inexperience will be revealed in the harsh, fluorescent light of your open-plan office.

Dear reader, in the final section of this book, I talk about how to manage yourself—that is, how to manage your own mindset and approach as a manager. I will discuss how to ensure that the new power you have is kept in check, how to manage your discomfort when you become the boss of a close friend, and how to manage decisions about your own career. I will also share how to manage your own boss.

The very fact that you are reading this book shows that you are a manager or soon-to-be manager who cares about your own self-growth and development. That's huge. It means you are committed to creating the best experience for your team members by committing to be the best manager you can be. *I* have no doubt that you are well on your way to becoming a great manager, and this next section will help *you* believe that as well. And as President Obama said in 2016, "I mean, you've got to have confidence . . . you got to be your own number one fan."[1]

So your first lesson in managing yourself: Believe that you belong in this crazy club of management. You're a manager for a reason. Be your own number one fan.

CHAPTER 22

CONFIDENCE AND VULNERABILITY

One of the best things about writing a book on management is that people send me tons of articles, stories, and YouTube clips on anything vaguely related to management. And I've actively solicited favorite management advice, asking a whole range of folks for their number one piece of management wisdom. To my question, "If you are going to be stranded on a deserted island and could take only one management nugget with you, what would it be?" tried and true answers came pouring in. "Share the praise; take the blame" and "People don't care how much you know until they know how much you care" and "People will forget what you said, people will forget what you did, but people will never forget how you made them feel" and "Always check that your fly is zipped before standing up in front of a team meeting" were all popular answers, among many other management clichés you might find on inspirational posters or at the bottom of one's email signature.[1]

But the one piece of advice that has stuck with me over the years came from my brilliant friend Tyler. When asked for the best piece of advice he received when he became a manager, Tyler said, "Show confidence up and vulnerability down."

I love this advice because it sums up so many important concepts to remember as a manager and because it feels counterintuitive—especially to new managers. First, this advice emphasizes the importance of managing "up," that is, managing your own manager. In chapter 24, I will tackle in depth how to manage your own manager effectively. Spoiler alert: To manage your manager, you need to show confidence in your ability to execute work, manage your team, and be a thought partner to your boss. You "show confidence up" by *owning* the relationship with your manager. You anticipate your manager's needs and take items off of your manager's plate without them asking. That's confidence.

Show confidence up and vulnerability down.

But what does "vulnerability down" mean? And why would you ever want to be vulnerable to the people you are leading, especially when your team knows you are new at this whole management rodeo? Won't they see weakness in your ability if you are vulnerable to them? Won't they respect you more if you show lots and lots of confidence in your abilities?

Well, two things. First, people are really good at sniffing out baloney. If you're a new manager, loads of confidence to your subordinates reeks of false bravado. People want a leader who has a clear direction but knows what they don't know, can ask for help, and is willing to listen to others. Too much confidence down ends up feeling like a dictatorship. And last time I checked, dictators tend to get toppled.

> People want a leader who has a clear direction
> but knows what they don't know, can ask for
> help, and is willing to listen to others.

And the second thing: vulnerability is critical to managing down because vulnerability builds trust. Vulnerability is when you show an openness to not knowing all of the answers all the time; or show that you are flawed and have weaknesses you are working on; or share when you have fears or anxieties about something. That's vulnerability. And trust is the secret sauce that improves communication, reduces bad types of conflict, makes people feel connected to a team, allows risk-taking and healthy mistakes, and encourages psychological safety and a whole bunch of other wonderful, magical things that just make work better.

I'm sure, dear reader, you are rolling your eyes: Vulnerability is the hot term these days in life and management. Plenty of speakers, academics, and armchair therapists have extolled its virtue. But here's the rub that's often missing from the loads of musings on vulnerability. For new managers, there's a risk of conflating incompetence with vulnerability. You try hard to be vulnerable, but your team sees incompetence. Vulnerability only works when it's coupled with competence. So what's the difference between incompetence and vulnerability? Let's dive in with some *slightly* fabricated scenarios.

Scenario 1

A manager I know, Christina, was asked to give a TED-like presentation to her entire organization. We discussed how the preparation for this TED Talk was a great way to be vulnerable with her team of eight. She prepared mightily for the presentation, and I had no doubt in my mind she was going to do an outstanding job (given her competence of the subject area). So how could she talk to her team about this presentation?

- Option 1: "I'm going to bomb this TED Talk. I didn't prepare at all."

- Option 2: "Public speaking still makes me really nervous despite giving lots of presentations. I still have to memorize every big presentation in order to be prepared."

Trust me: at some point, we all fall into the option 1 framing (recall the I-didn't-study-for-the-final-at-all, I'm-going-to-totally-fail line many of us used in college). Option 1 conveys incompetence (and in this case, inauthentic incompetence). But option 2 shows vulnerability. It lets

Christina's team know that even the best public speakers still get epic nerves.

Scenario 2

Another manager I worked with, Fatima, was about to talk to her team about potential layoffs that were coming down the pike. Fatima was scared for her own job and didn't know what was going to happen to her, let alone the rest of the team. Her team was asking questions about the uncertainty that seemed to hang in the air and was looking to her for answers. How should Fatima frame this news with her team?

- Option 1: "Hey, guys. I'm in the dark just as much as you all and am also petrified about losing my job. I have no idea what's going on."

- Option 2: "Hey, guys. I'm also anxious about the uncertainty that's going on around here. It's really scary trying to make decisions and navigate our day-to-day when it's not yet clear exactly what's going to happen. I'm going to try to get answers for our team as soon as humanly possible."

In option 1, it might feel like Fatima is building lots of trust because she's being vulnerable about losing her job and building empathy with what her team is experiencing. But people will immediately think that Fatima is so worried about her own job that she can't worry about making the best decisions about the future of each of her team members. The team will code the manager as incompetent: She doesn't have any control over the situation. Option 2 allows Fatima to acknowledge the uncertainty that is coming and why it's challenging to navigate it. She also shares the actions she is taking to support the team.

Vulnerability as a manager often means saying, "I don't know," or, "Let me find out more information," when a team member asks a question that you don't know the answer to. It often means admitting when you made a mistake or sharing how you could have done better. And it often means sharing that a situation you might find yourself in is a totally new one, and the challenges you are facing are not ones that you've had to confront before.

Often as a new manager, you aim to have all of the answers before you stand in front of your team. But this may come back to bite you. You can never have all of the answers or be an expert in everything. In my coaching, I do lots of role plays with new managers. We practice a difficult conversation with an employee, and frequently the manager will ask me, "What do I say if my employee asks X?" and X is an impossible question without a clear answer. It's difficult for the manager to accept that "I don't know" may be a perfectly appropriate response to the employee's question. At times, the manager refuses to have the difficult and necessary conversation because they don't have the answers to all of the potential questions that the employee *might* ask. We will never know all the answers. Get used to saying "I don't know."

And what's at risk if you *don't* show vulnerability and don't admit when you've made a mistake or chosen the wrong path? You become defensive and impenetrable. You don't seek out situations that might cause discomfort. Your team avoids hurting your feelings or saying something that disagrees with your approach (because if you can't own up to being wrong, then why would anyone ever point that out to you?). Your defensiveness and failure to admit faults in your own self fuels a team that is disempowered and not inclusive.[2] So show some darn vulnerability.

It's hard being vulnerable, whether in your personal life or at work. It takes a ton of courage, but the benefits are huge. Earlier in the book, I briefly shared a story from my teaching that helps to illustrate this point. Let me expand. Many years ago, I was teaching a class of about thirty graduate students. The class got into a raw discussion and some students took big social risks by sharing personal stories. In the past, I always played the role of the facilitator and stayed on the outside of these conversations. But for some reason, the conversation touched me in a way I didn't expect. I shared a personal story of my own . . . and I started to cry. In front of a class of thirty students. As a female, relatively young teacher. There was no hiding the raw vulnerability of the moment. It was petrifying and I felt like the semester of strong teaching, gravitas, rapport, and respect I had worked so hard to build was about to completely evaporate.

> **It's hard being vulnerable, whether in your personal life or at work. It takes a ton of courage, but the benefits are huge.**

But the total opposite happened. The class became closer to me and I to them. They rallied around me. We developed a level of trust that other classes in the past didn't experience. The students didn't doubt my competence after my display of vulnerability. Trust me: crying in front of a class is pretty low on my list of things I enjoy doing. But in that moment, it was an authentic expression that bridged the divide between student and teacher.

So it's pretty simple when you sum it all up: to be a great manager, show confidence up and vulnerability down.

TL;DR

- Best management advice I've received? Show confidence up and vulnerability down.

- You show confidence to your manager through owning your relationship and anticipating your manager's needs.

- Vulnerability is the openness to admitting you're wrong, and sharing what you feel or what scares you.

- Vulnerability allows for trust building and for authenticity. Both have huge benefits to your team and to you.

- But it's important to make sure you're not confusing incompetence with vulnerability, especially as a new manager.

CHAPTER 23

POWER: USE IT FOR GOOD, NOT EVIL

Here's the story: You're out on a Thursday night with close friends from work. You're having your beverage of choice and having a great time. You're all talking about work, about the weekend hiking trip you're all going on, and perhaps about who is dating whom at the company. Your start-up is all consuming, but at the end of the day, you feel lucky that you're working with a bunch of people you adore and who you call friends.

Friday morning comes. Promotions are announced. Score! You've been promoted. Super exciting until you hear that you are now managing a close friend. The friend who you hang out with all the time and were hanging out with last night. The friend who has seen the tears, the anger, and the joy that you've expressed about your job over the last few years.

There's a lot of discomfort that comes from being a manager. You give constructive feedback that you know may not be well-received. You make decisions that your team is not happy with. You fire a team member who everyone loves but who is underperforming. As a manager, you find yourself navigating lots of situations that are downright uncomfortable. One of the most awkward situations that new managers face is managing a friend. In extreme cases, as illustrated above, you may be put in the position of managing a close friend who is the same age and tenure as you. In a less extreme case, you may end up managing team members who you really like. You struggle with the gnarliness of having authority over someone with whom you are personally close.

What typically happens when you manage a friend? In my experience, I see two things go down:

1. You become very bossy and official. You try to act in a buttoned-up and corporate way, and as such, you go way too far down the path of being a manator (manator: (*noun*) a manager dictator. Synonyms: despboss, manacrat, bosspressor).

2. You become incredibly deferential to the friend you are managing. You don't want to step on toes for fear of harming the friendship, and you never state what you need or expect from the relationship.

"Friend" and "manager" do not need to be mutually exclusive states. But navigating the friend and manager relationship does require both a deep understanding of yourself and empathy and discipline in how you approach the relationship.

> **"Friend" and "manager" do not need to be mutually exclusive states.**

Let's first talk about what happens when you become a manager. When you become a manager, you gain power. You gain the explicit power to make certain decisions, structure work in a particular way, and influence how your group operates. You also gain implicit power because of your new status as a manager. Team members may defer to you because of your position and look to you for answers and guidance. So as a manager you have more power than you had before.

But why, you might ask, does it matter that you gain power as a manager? And why does it matter when managing a friend? It matters because power can subconsciously push you to act in a way that is not aligned with being a great manager. Whether you like it or not, power corrupts you. Your friends may be justified in their worry when you start to manage them.

You need to understand what happens when you gain power, so that you can *consciously* push against these actions. Here are some things that happen when you're in power:

- You protect your power. When you are in power you have a natural tendency to try to stay in power, so you protect your own interests (as opposed to sharing with your team).[1]

- You are more likely to listen to information and opinions from team members who are like you, as opposed to those who have expertise or relevant knowledge. Put another way, when you get more powerful, you favor people who look and act like you![2]

- You act with fewer constraints and you have greater freedom to act at will.[3]

- Furthermore, if your team feels that there is a large power differential, they may be less willing to take risks and the team may end up having lower overall psychological safety (as we discussed in chapter 18).

So first thing to realize when you're managing a friend: You might be acting like a totally different person because of the power you now have. Be aware of this.

Okay, you might start to behave differently when you get power. But what else is challenging about managing a friend? Researchers Elinor Amit and Joshua Greene found that when we are socially close to someone, we are less objective and more emotional in our decision-making.[4] Yikes.

INVERSE RELATIONSHIPS OF THE INFLATING HEAD AKA THE "WHAT POWER DOES TO US" GRAPH

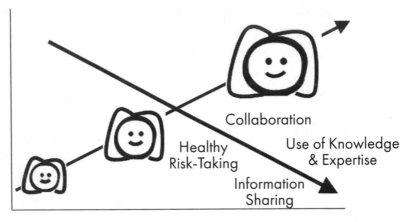

Collaboration

Healthy
Risk-Taking

Use of Knowledge
& Expertise

Information
Sharing

INCREASING POWER

So this means that when you manage a friend, you might throw rational decision-making aside. You might ignore data. Your clear-headed, calm approach to management may go totally out the window. Couple this finding with the other ways power wreaks havoc on your ability to manage, and it's not surprising that your friend goes running for the hills when you start to manage them.

When your coworker is no longer just a friend, here are some techniques to focus on building a great friend–manager relationship:

- **Acknowledge the awkwardness.** First things first, have a conversation with your friend that you feel a little awkward being put in this position but that you know you guys can make it work. Just put it out there that it's weird. Ask how your friend is feeling. Come back to this conversation over time.

- **Don't forget about expectations.** But after you acknowledge the awkwardness, work to jointly develop a set of norms for how you're going to approach the manager–team member relationship. Set expectations upfront of how you want to work together and how you want to communicate. Obviously, all managers should do this, but it's especially important as you are navigating a more complex relationship.

- **Remember what your role is as a manager.** It's not to tell people what to do. It's to motivate, communicate, help structure work, and develop. You can frame the relationship as a partnership, and lean on your team member as a partner, not as someone who does your bidding. Lead with, "What can I do to help you in your job?" Think about what you can do to make your team member/friend's work life easier. You'll be even more excited to help because you care about this person on another level.

- **Show vulnerability while having confidence that you were promoted for a reason.** Managing a friend incites the most severe case of impostor syndrome possible. You're already feeling queasy that you're not ready to be a manager *and* your friend knows you really well. Therefore, you fear that your friend can *see right through you.* Don't question or undermine the decision that made you a manager but do share and be open with your friend that there's a lot that you need to learn and will work on developing.

- **Don't be afraid of giving constructive feedback** but be careful the feedback doesn't get personal. Try really hard to give frequent feedback to your friend, and more importantly, encourage your friend to do the same. The sooner you can make feedback an unemotional activity that you do as part of your work, the better. If you wait to give feedback until you're frustrated, it's going to be far worse, far more emotional, and far more hurtful to your relationship.

- **Watch your mouth.** Be hyper-aware of your language choices when you're managing a friend. Be careful about creating a separation between you and your friend when you communicate. For example, don't use the royal "we" (e.g., "We think you'll be ready for a promotion in six months") or other words that put you in a different tier from your friend. It feels impersonal and underhandedly exclusionary. Language matters.

At the end of the day, the qualities of a good friend—empathy, patience, wanting the best for the other person, and compassionate honesty—are also the qualities of a great manager.

> The qualities of a good friend—empathy, patience, wanting the best for the other person, and compassionate honesty—are also the qualities of a great manager.

TL;DR

- We often have to manage people with whom we are socially close. Particularly in start-ups, we may be in the position of managing a close friend.

- When we're put in a position of power, we may end up changing our behavior subconsciously. This includes seeking input from and showing favoritism toward those who are most similar to us, not those who are most qualified or knowledgeable.

- Additionally, our teams may be less likely to take risks or less likely to share information when we gain authority.

- To effectively manage a friend, you should start by acknowledging that you feel awkward in your new position and solicit your friend's help in defining and structuring the managerial relationship.

- Additionally, you should use great general manager hygiene, including setting expectations and providing constructive, compassionate feedback.

CHAPTER 24

MANAGING UP

L et me tell you a little story about a weekly ritual I had at my last start-up. On Tuesday mornings at 9:00 a.m., I had a standing meeting with my boss, Samaiyah. And every Monday night, I would go through a little dance. I would dance through a set of five options for how to approach that darn Tuesday morning meeting.

Option 1, which I deployed approximately 40 percent of the time, involved canceling the Tuesday meeting on Monday night, and in the cancellation write a breezy note: "Nothing new going on—let's chat next week!! :)"

Option 2, a variation of option 1, involved canceling the meeting with no note and no notification and hoping that Samaiyah, in all of her busyness, didn't notice that the meeting invitation magically disappeared. This was, by far, my favorite option, but one that I could only deploy sparingly.

Option 3 required a little planning on Monday night. It involved coming up with a work "crisis" that I could chat about during our meeting and seek my boss's wise counsel on. This had the added benefit of making Samaiyah feel very useful and smart. It also hid the fact that I had nothing else to talk about. Option 3 was the second most-used option, and every so often actually led to an interesting conversation.

Option 4—the gossip option—was by far the most fun but also risky. It involved starting the meeting with a bunch of questions about Samaiyah's dating life, new puppy, and weekend plans, and then pivoting into a question of "Did you hear about so-and-so?" The hope was that she would take the bait and either blab about her last date or chat about another coworker until the time ran out of our meeting. (Note, dear reader, I am not *proud* of this option, I am just sharing what went down.)

And then, of course, option 5 was a Hail Mary pass. I showed up at the meeting with nothing and hoped that Samaiyah had something she wanted to discuss with me.

Managing up—or managing *your* boss—is a key but often overlooked part of what it takes for *you* to be a great manager. The standing manager meeting that I reference above (also called the "one-on-one," or the "check-in," among other ambiguous and anxicty-provoking terms) is the absolutely perfect example of everything that is challenging about managing up: You don't really know what you're supposed to use your boss for, you don't know who should be leading these interactions, you don't know how much to expose yourself in terms of challenges you're facing, and you don't actually know what your boss wants out of you (partly because your boss never read chapter 1 of this book!).

> **Managing up—or managing your boss—**
> **is a key but often overlooked part of what it**
> **takes for you to be a great manager.**

But why, you might ask, is managing up an important part of learning how to manage your own team? As a manager, you are responsible for the development and day-to-day structure of another individual—and poorly managing up can wreak havoc on those you manage. How often do you begrudgingly task your team member with something you don't agree with but that your boss suggests? Or how often do you not have any rational explanation for a decision that affects your team member other than, "*My* boss told me to do it"? When you don't manage up effectively, you run the risk of potentially undermining your own authority in the eyes of your team. It becomes impossible for you to manage down well when you can't manage up well.

Let's talk about what makes it challenging to manage up.

THE COLLISION OF THE COGNITIVE LOAD AND THE SPOTLIGHT EFFECT

Cognitive Load Theory focuses on how humans process and store information.[1] Lots of new information increases one's cognitive load, that is, how much information you are managing in your brain. The increase in cognitive load in turn reduces the functioning of one's short-term working memory. Bluntly, your memory works worse when tons and tons of "stuff" is piled on. You may have experienced this phenomenon when on the day you have a million things going on, you lose your house keys. And given that the typical CEO gets about three hundred emails per day and has to make countless decisions, the cognitive load of a boss is quite high (and, thus, her short-term memory can be quickly compromised).

The Spotlight Effect is one of the more humbling psychological theories (especially for the only children out there, sorry guys) as it talks about our own egocentrism.[2] Essentially, we think people notice us more than they actually do, but people aren't noticing us because they are too busy thinking about themselves and thinking that others are noticing them (and the loop continues). Therefore, because we are the centers of our own work universe and think about our work all the time, we have a biased sense of how much our bosses think about us and the work that we are doing.

In short, our bosses have a hard time mentally juggling multiple things, especially items requiring short-term working memory. And we tend to overweigh our own importance in the eyes of others. We think our bosses think about us all the time and think about the projects we are working on. Not only are our bosses *not* thinking about us all the time, but our bosses are mentally swamped and can't even remember what we are working on.

THE SPOTLIGHT EFFECT TAKES ON THE COGNITIVE LOAD

THE EXPERT INFLECTION POINT

It's likely that your first manager knew way more than you. They knew more about how to get work done well, about the company's product, about your functional area, and about the industry. You looked to your boss for answers as they were an expert and you were not. For you newer managers out there, I'm going to venture a guess and say that this is how your team members look at you. As a new manager, you have likely been promoted because you are an expert at what you are now managing. You are great at marketing, so you are managing a team of marketers. You are a black belt Excel modeler, so you now have a team of finance minions building models for you. Your team comes to you for answers because you know more than them.

Well, there comes a time when you know more than your boss about your functional area. This is what I call the manager-expert inflection point. It's the point in your career when you are more of an expert than your boss. Think about it. The chief operating officer of a company is not the smartest legal mind, or finance mind, or compliance mind in the company. But those brilliant minds all report into the COO. The VP of

THE MANAGER-EXPERT
INFLECTION POINT

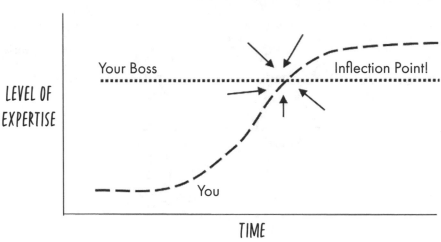

legal knows far more about law than the COO, but the COO still manages the VP of legal.

An important part of managing up is recognizing and embracing when you've hit the manager-expert inflection point. You will approach your conversations and your meetings with your boss from a completely different perspective. You will not look to your boss for all the answers; rather, you might look to your boss for information about how your work connects cross-functionally, or how a problem you are trying to solve aligns with the other priorities in your boss's purview. Your boss becomes a thought partner instead of just an answerer to every question you have. You have the responsibility of being the expert and making sure your boss has all the information they need to do their job (while not overloading them with unnecessary information).

To manage up well, you need to account for the collision of the cognitive load with the spotlight effect, and you need to embrace the expert inflection point. *How* do you manage up well?

THE TWO ABSOLUTE MOST IMPORTANT THINGS YOU NEED TO DO TO MANAGE UP

1. **Own the execution of the relationship.** Take charge of every aspect in the relationship with your boss.
   - Own the **tactical** aspects of your relationship: Come to every meeting with an agenda (better yet, send the agenda in advance), tell your boss what you want to talk about and drive the meeting, ask for what you need (including constructive feedback), and overly communicate progress, deliverables, and timing. Never wait for your boss to ask for an update on a project—proactively provide that information.

   - Own the **strategic** aspects of your relationship (i.e., own the "thinking"): Anticipate the needs of your boss, and when possible, have your boss react to a set of solutions, not a set of problems you have. Every boss *loves* the conversation with a team member that goes like this: "Hey, boss, I've run into problem A, and here are the three options we have to address it—what do you think?"

2. **Understand and adapt to your boss's style.** Support your boss's ability to be as successful as possible.
   - Understand what your boss needs to be successful and commit to your boss's success. You're on the same team as your boss; make sure they know that. Always have your boss's back, provide open and constructive feedback to your manager, and learn what they need to be successful in their role.

   - Figure out how to complement your boss's style, as opposed to expecting that you and your boss will have an identical style of working—or worse yet, expecting that your boss will adapt to your style. You're going to work for a number of different bosses throughout your career; as such, learn how to adapt your own style to complement the style of your current boss (i.e., build the "skill" of adaptability).

- For example, if your boss is supremely disorganized, don't spend all of your time bemoaning the fact that they are a hot mess; rather, think about how you can bring order and structure to the relationship.

- Some of the most rewarding boss relationships I've had are with those bosses who are wildly different from me. At first it was disorienting and frustrating to work for a boss who had a different philosophy or approach to our work. But once I realized that it actually provided me a huge opportunity to fill in the gaps of my boss, it was incredibly rewarding.

So, dear reader, to be a great manager, you have to get great at managing your own boss. And to do that, you have to help reduce your boss's cognitive load by being proactive and owning the relationship. And you have to learn how to be adaptive and complement your manager's style (and future managers' styles). When you manage up well, you'll be a role model for your team as well. Which, of course, means your cognitive load will be reduced and no one will ever secretly cancel their one-on-one meetings with you.

TL;DR

- Managing up—that is, managing your own boss—is an important but often overlooked part of being a great manager.

- It's hard to manage up because we think our bosses spend more time thinking about us than they actually do—and because of the number of activities and decisions they have to make, they might even forget what we're doing.

- It's also hard because we expect our boss to be an expert in our work, but over time we become the expert and it is our responsibility to inform our boss.

- To manage up well, you first need to own the execution of the relationship, which means you should direct and drive every tactical and strategic aspect of the work you do with your boss.

- You also need to adapt to your manager's style by complementing where your boss falls short. You'll be an invaluable resource and build a stronger partnership with your boss.

CHAPTER 25

SHOULD I STAY, OR SHOULD I GO?

Dear reader, we are coming to the end of our management journey. And like all good journeys, there is often a point when you are forced to make a decision, determine which path you want to go down, and choose your own adventure. Because you have read this book and utilized all of the techniques discussed, you are a great manager, beloved by all your team members. Therefore, you are attractive to other companies. Inevitably, you will one day be recruited to join another organization and will have to contemplate whether to stay where you are or go someplace new.

I once was headhunted to join a fast-growing, well-funded start-up, and the opportunity seemed too good to pass up, despite the fact that I hadn't been looking to leave my current role.[1] My boss at the time, Diana, a seasoned CEO, took the information in stride when I mentioned that I was contemplating a move. Upon hearing my choice to stay or go, she provided incredible advice.

Diana said, "The beauty of getting an unsolicited job offer is that it forces you to step back and think through three different outcomes. It causes you to think:

1. 'Actually, I really like my current role, but there are things in this role that I want to fix or change moving forward to make this role work for the long term.'

2. 'Wow, this new offer is exactly what I want to do, and I'm going to go forward with it.'

3. 'This job offer isn't exactly what I want, but it makes me realize that I do want to look for other jobs outside my company.'"

Beyond just a lesson in how to respond with grace and generosity when one of your employees comes to you with a big life decision, I love this advice because of what it highlights about how you manage yourself through a difficult leaving decision.

I'm a person who is highly susceptible to flattery. So receiving an unsolicited job offer played right into that weakness. Despite Diana's fantastic advice, I didn't fully consider option 3. I knew that my current role wasn't for me in the long term (option 1), and it was too hard to pass up an opportunity that had found me (option 2). The offer-in-hand had certainty and a clear timeline. I was going from one certain outcome (my current role) to a new certain outcome (a new role). Option 3 was off the table.

In hindsight, option 3 might have been the right choice. But why is it hard to go with option 3? In chapter 13, I talk about the status quo bias: The innate desire for us to stay with what we know and what's certain. But that would imply that we would never go with option 2, and we know that people change jobs all the time. The primary reason why it's hard to evaluate option 3 is because of the streetlight effect (also known colloquially as the drunkard's search principle). And you guessed it—the streetlight effect is yet another cognitive bias. You are biased in how you search: You search for things where it is easiest to look (for example, you search for your lost car keys right under a streetlight as opposed to other parts of a dark street).

Options 1 and 2 are right under the streetlight. The option 3 jobs—though they may be filled with rainbows and butterflies and unicorns—are in the dark, so you don't evaluate them.

THE STREETLIGHT EFFECT AS APPLIED TO YOUR JOB SEARCH

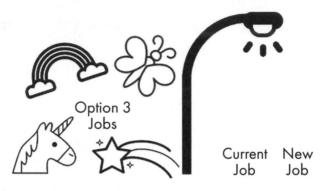

Option 3
Jobs

Current   New
Job   Job

How can you manage yourself to think through option 3 when evaluating job offers? And how can you evaluate option 3 when you are swamped with your day-to-day job and just don't have the mental space to be proactive?

To properly build the muscle to one day evaluate option 3, you need to start now. The challenge of option 3 is that it sneaks up on you when you're not looking for it. You might not be actively searching for a job when you are presented with this job dilemma. So I suggest breaking things down into microsteps, and start working through these small snackable tasks that make the whole job-search-when-you-really-don't-want-to-be-job-searching process a bit more palatable.

The Clash ask: "Should I stay, or should I go?" But all good karaokers know that the second verse of this iconic song asks, "Should I stay, or should I go *now*?" Here is a list of tasks that help you to evaluate what you need in your next role to determine if the answer to the second verse is: "I should go *later*."

THE LUNCHABLES APPROACH TO FIGURING OUT YOUR NEXT ROLE

THE INTENTION STATEMENT

At the beginning of every yoga class, there are a few seconds of intention setting: why you're in the class that day and what you're hoping to accomplish. It's a lovely exercise in creating a small bit of space to be thoughtful instead of just barreling forward with the next activity.

To start out this quasi job search, set an intention for the search, and more importantly, for the next step in your career. In a few sentences, write out why you're embarking on this process (e.g., could be what you're missing in your current role), what you're hoping to achieve, and what you're looking for in your next role or next step.

MAD LIBS JOB DIMENSIONS

Like a life partner, every job is filled with a set of compromises and deal breakers. Yet we often don't explicitly think through all of the dimensions of a job and what is most important to us at each step in our careers.

Step through each dimension of a job—role, organization, life needs—and write down what you want in each. Some dimensions won't matter, but others will (e.g., you don't care if you work in the health-care industry or the education sector, but it's really important that you work for a small company). Once you've gone through each dimension, choose your deal breakers—those dimensions you must have in your next role.

See template in the appendix to support this exercise.

THE ENVY LIST

Don't get me wrong. I'm quite happy with my role as writer, coach, and board advisor. Yet I have one friend whose job I am insanely jealous of—she works for a cool company, has a small awesome team, gets ridiculous travel perks, and has a sweet compensation package. I find it helpful to think through why I am jealous of her role and what components of it I could incorporate into my current or future work.

For your envy list, make a list of five people whose jobs you envy. And for those people you know, grab a coffee with them and ask to learn more about what they do, what their favorite parts about their job are, and what their least favorites are.

THE ELEVATOR PITCH

Start to jot down what your ideal job would look like using what you learned from the envy list and the mad libs exercise. Distill the description of your ideal job into a single paragraph that you can share with others (you can get into more detail later—keep this one simple).

For example: "I'm looking for an operations role on the leadership team of a small and scaling start-up (Series A or B) in the Austin area in the fintech space. I'm looking to bring my past experience in finance, operations, legal, and HR to lead these functions in the organization."

THE STRENGTH OF WEAK TIES LIST

Research shows that you'll likely get a job through your "weak ties"—your friends of friends.[2] We often ask our immediate network if they know of any roles that would be interesting to us. Instead, ask your immediate network to put you in touch with interesting people.

Your microstep is to email fifteen close friends or colleagues stating that you are exploring other roles (include your elevator pitch) and ask them to introduce you to three or four of their friends who they think would have an interesting perspective to share. (Being specific is key: Don't say, "Do you know any interesting people?" Rather, ask "Could you introduce me to three friends in this field . . . ?")

One suggestion when you are tackling these activities: Give yourself one small task to do each week. Don't think about the next task on the list or try to do all at once. Research shows that "precrastinators" (those of us who, when assigned a task, immediately want to check it off of our list) could benefit from going a bit slower.[3] Going slowly through these tasks is beneficial: It allows what you learn each week to marinate and update subsequent steps.

Of course, updating your résumé, cleaning up a cover letter, and speaking to recruiters, among other things, are also important parts to a job search. While you're at it, you may want to do some job crafting (as we discussed in chapter 3) on your current role to better understand areas where you could grow and develop without moving. This particular list of microsteps is meant to get you thinking and expand your awareness of what other roles are out there. It's meant for you to be thoughtful and holistic about what you want and need in your next role. You'll be more prepared to evaluate option 3 and all the rainbows, butterflies, and unicorns it may provide when a job offer falls in your lap.

TL;DR

- A job offer is helpful in pushing you to think about if you want to stay in your current role, if you want to take the new role, or if you want to look for another role outside of your current company.

- There are a number of small steps you can take to better inform what you want and need in a new role, and how you can start to build a network of people who could support you in finding a new role.

- These steps include setting an intention; clearly articulating job dimensions and prioritizing those that are most important to you; honing an elevator pitch; and listing people who can support you in this process.

- These are called microsteps for a reason. The idea is to tackle one at a time and let the learnings from each step inform the next step.

A FINAL NOTE ON MANAGING YOURSELF

A number of years ago, one of my most favorite team members I've ever managed, Kathryn, was finally leaving her job for an exciting new role. She wrote me a lovely card thanking me for supporting her career over the years. In this card, Kathryn shared what she thought was the best piece of advice I had ever given her during our time working together. I immediately assumed the advice was going to be about managing complex organizations, or how to think strategically early in your career, or how to navigate a start-up while remaining sane. Nope. Not even close. Of all the wise advice I had bestowed upon her, the piece Kathryn found most impactful was, "Don't love something that can't love you back."

Don't love something that can't love you back.

In leaving our start-up, Kathryn experienced what you will likely face at some point in your career. You fall in love with your organization, give it your absolute all, and create an identity around your role and value in the company. You pour your heart and soul into the people you manage and put your company above most other things in your life. But then you don't get the promotion you expect or don't get the raise that you feel would reward you for being so devoted to your work. And you are devastated. How could something you love so much not reciprocate those same feelings?

I gave Kathryn this advice when she was struggling with whether to look for a new job. She had grown significantly, and there wasn't a role in our organization that would challenge her in the way she needed for her long-term career. Kathryn's cognitive dissonance was strong: How could she possibly leave something that she loved and that was such a big part of her identity?

As I've discussed in these final chapters, an important part of being a great manager is managing yourself. And as I discussed in chapter 1, managing expectations—in this case, managing your *own* expectations about your role within your organization—is critical to managing yourself. Thus, to be a great manager, be loyal, be committed, be hard-working, and love your colleagues, but don't love something that can't love you back. Understand that your organization may change and it may one day outgrow you (and you might outgrow it). This means understanding that your organization cannot "love you" like your partner, mother, dog, or cat (scratch that—no cat actually loves its owner).

WHAT TO LOVE

Your Team

Your Dog

Your Mom

WHAT NOT TO LOVE

Your Company

As I'm sure you have already experienced, being a manager is an emotionally and intellectually taxing job. You are responsible for the development and careers of others, and your actions have a direct impact on how someone experiences their day. Being a manager is also one of the most rewarding things you can do. You build deep relationships with your team members and help shepherd them through pivotal moments in their careers and life.

> Being a manager is an emotionally and intellectually taxing job . . . Being a manager is also one of the most rewarding things you can do.

It's important to maintain some distance and equanimity when you are on this management journey, else both the emotional and intellectual weight will take a toll on you. And there is a way to be wholly committed to your team and the people you manage, while also taking care of your needs and your own career. But what does this mean in practice?

For you, this means building skills, capabilities, and commitment within your current role while always ensuring that you have choices and are open to opportunities outside that role. This may mean leaving your company despite loving and being loyal to the people you work with. This also means making hard decisions about a loyal, kind underperformer, and being excited and supportive about a high-performing team member who chooses to leave your organization.

Dear reader, I have no doubt that you are a committed, loyal, hard-working manager. You seek to do the best for and by your team. You give your whole self to your work and your role, and your team greatly benefits from your desire to be a great manager. But please remember this advice as you continue to navigate this wild management journey: don't love something that can't love you back.

APPENDIX

EXPECTATION-SETTING TEMPLATE

FOUR PRONGS	MORE INFO PLEASE	DETAILS
1. What's the objective or end goal?	Why do you need or want this? What are we trying to achieve through this work? What impact will it have on you and on the client or customer?	
2. What does good look like?	What defines success for this activity or deliverable? How specific can you be about what a quality product looks like?	
3. What's the timing?	When do you need the output by? When do you want to see a first draft? In what state?	
4. What are examples, if possible?	Share other work product, information, or content to support employee.	

INDIVIDUAL DEVELOPMENT PLAN TEMPLATE

1. ONE-YEAR GOALS
What are your career goals over the next year at X in general? What role do you hope to play at X by the end of the year? How do you hope to be viewed by your fellow employees?

2. THREE-YEAR (LONGER-TERM) GOALS
What are your long-term career goals? Where do you see yourself in three years? What title or role do you hope to achieve within X? What do you hope to achieve outside of X?

3. CAPABILITIES/SKILLS			
What are the three capabilities or skills you want to build over this year?	What are the activities, projects, or training you will do to build this skill or capability you identified? Be as specific as possible.	How will you measure success? What tangible outcome or metric will measure your improvement?	Who will support you in building this capability?

POWERFUL COACHING QUESTIONS

COACHING QUESTIONS	
What's exciting about this option?	What have you tried so far?
What does your gut tell you about the situation?	What led to this situation?
Where is the urgency coming from?	If you could wave a magic wand, what would the situation look like?
How do you feel about the situation?	What will you start doing tomorrow?
What's not yet clear about what's going on? How could you get clarity?	How do you explain this situation to yourself? To a friend?
What else is there for you?	What have you learned about yourself through this situation?
What's the challenge here? What do you find most challenging?	What will you do differently in the future when a similar situation arises?
What would that outcome look like?	What's at risk if you don't take action?
What other options have you not explored?	What's at risk if you do take action?
What's another possible way to address this?	What does no action look like?
What would you do differently if you could have a do-over?	What concerns you most about the situation?
What do you want out of this situation?	What do you fear about the situation?
What's the ideal outcome?	What is preventing you from taking action?
What's the next best possible outcome?	What information or support do you need to decide?

(Questions adapted from *Co-Active Coaching Toolkit*)

PERFORMANCE IMPROVEMENT PLAN TEMPLATE

TEAM MEMBER NAME:	MANAGER:
ROLE:	DATE OF PLAN:
LENGTH OF PIP:	
Overview of Performance Improvement Plan *Where has the team member not met expectations?*	

Areas of Improvement: To be a full contributor to the team, we see X primary areas of improvement. Under each area of improvement, we have outlined examples of where expectations have not been met in this area.

AREAS OF IMPROVEMENT	EXAMPLE(S)

Plan Moving Forward: To help you improve the areas above, we propose you focus on the following areas over the next X weeks. We have outlined key objectives of each of these areas, as well as the expectations for timing and deliverables. Again, we will evaluate progress on these areas [during the week of X].

KEY ACTIVITIES	ADDITIONAL DETAILS	TIMING

MOTIVATION INTAKE FORM

MOTIVATION INTAKE FORM	
How do you like to receive feedback?	
What's your biggest motivator in your job? In your career?	
What type of work gets you most excited? Why?	
What specific type of work do you struggle with executing? Why?	
Anything else I should know about how you like to work?	

COMPETENCY MATRIX TEMPLATE

For each level of your organization, identify the key competencies that an employee should master. Add columns to reflect additional categories of competency (e.g., Client Relationship Skills; Functional Skills). For the next level, the prior level competencies apply and new competencies also are put in place.

EMPLOYEE LEVEL	ROLE DESCRIPTION	SCOPE OF ROLE	MASTERY	LEADERSHIP
e.g., analyst	e.g., conducts research and analyzes specific business problems, including market and competitive analysis	e.g., supports team in executing clearly defined projects and deliverables; acts proactively to best support the research team	e.g., successfully demonstrates analytical skills on client projects; demonstrated ability to work with large datasets and Excel	e.g., contributes to internal team initiatives; proactive member of the team; mentors new team members and interns
e.g., senior analyst				

INTERVIEW PROCESS TEMPLATE

The objective is for all candidates to go through the same process. This is a sample process and should be adapted.

STEP 1: SCREENING	STEP 2: ONSITE INTERVIEW	STEP 3: WORK ASSESSMENT/ LEADERSHIP SIMULATION	STEP 4: OFFER AND ONBOARDING
1. Role definition: Develop high-level job description and key capabilities that are "must-haves" in role.	**1. Interview One:** General Interview	**1. Additional interviews** or conversations with team members as needed.	**1. Offer negotiation** and offer extended to candidate.
2. Résumé screening	**2. Interview Two:** Functional Interview	**2. References:** Team conducts 2–3 references (formal or informal) of candidate.	**2. Employee guide** sent to provide overview of company policies.
3. First phone screen a. Test general interest, background, applicability to role. b. Share salary and other key expectations (e.g., geography) to ensure alignment before moving forward in process.	**3. Interview Three:** Behavioral Interview & Assessment	**3. Leadership Simulation/Work Assessment:** a. If possible, assessment should be conducted against multiple candidates in same time period. b. Team comes together immediately after to decide.	**3. Onboarding begins**
4. Second phone interview a. Test leadership skills, functional expertise, cultural fit.	**4. Evaluation:** a. Rate candidate across each dimension prior to group discussion with other interviewers b. Force rank candidates against each other		

AFFINITY BIAS EXERCISE

The affinity bias exercise, also called the circle of trust exercise, is a great way to help people recognize their potential unconscious biases and demonstrate the affinity bias that most of us experience. It is not clear who originally developed this exercise, but it is frequently used in organizations to highlight our subconscious biases.

Using the template, each team member writes down the names of the five people she trusts most deeply. Then, under each column the team member reflects the diversity of the five people she trusts most deeply (e.g., "F" for female under gender).

Once the grid is filled out, ask your team members to reflect on what they've written down. Ask them to share what they observe or what they noticed in going through this process.

FIVE MOST TRUSTED PEOPLE	GENDER	AGE	EDUCATION	SEXUAL ORIENTATION	DISABILITY	ETHNICITY/ RACE	SOCIOECONOMIC STATUS	OTHER

BEHAVIORAL INTERVIEW QUESTIONS

CAPABILITY	QUESTIONS
Results Orientation	What single project or task would you consider your most significant career accomplishment to date? Walk me through the plan, how you managed it, how you measured its success, and what the biggest mistakes you made were.
	Tell me about the project you led that had the greatest impact on your organization.
	Please describe an instance when you discovered an unexpected obstacle. How did you remove that barrier to still meet or exceed your goal?
Get-the-Job-Done Mentality	Tell me about an initiative you have taken to improve procedures at work. Were you successful? Would you do anything different now?
	Tell me about a time when you failed to meet a commitment you had made. What happened and why do you think it happened?
	How do you hold yourself accountable to your goals? How do you hold your team accountable to their goals? Tell me about a recent instance when your team didn't meet their goals.
EQ/Humility	Looking back, what has been your greatest professional lesson? Tell me about how it affected future decision-making/the way you work.
	Tell me about the worst manager or worst executive you've worked for. Why was this person so bad and what did you do about it?
	What skills or capabilities are you currently working on developing? How are you developing these? When have you leveraged colleagues to compensate for these areas of development?
	What has been the hardest interpersonal challenge you've faced in your job?

CAPABILITY	QUESTIONS
"Downward" Orientation	As you think about your career, who is a team member you had a huge impact on and what is she doing today as a result of your leadership or management of her? Tell me about a time when you broke a rule for an employee. Why? What was the outcome?
Leadership	Tell me about your style as a leader and use an example of how that comes to play in an executive team meeting. Describe a situation where you had to accomplish a challenging goal through influence rather than control. How satisfying or dissatisfying was this situation? What has been the most challenging leadership crisis you've experienced? How did you handle it and how did it change the way you lead?
Feedback & Willingness to Dissent	What has been the worst criticism you've received over the course of your career? How has this changed how you operate today? Tell me about a time when you didn't agree with the decision of your CEO/manager. Why didn't you agree and what did you do? What feedback do you have on the interview process thus far? What would you change?
Mission Orientation	Tell me about a time when you disagreed with the CEO because an initiative or activity didn't align with the mission of the organization. What did you do? What was the outcome? What are the values of your current organization (or most recent organization)? How do you specifically espouse those values on a day-to-day basis?
Team Management	Have you had to lay off or fire an employee? What were the circumstances and what was the outcome? Tell me about a time when you led a team that was dysfunctional or had dysfunctional tendencies. What was a specific change you made or implemented to help right the group? What is the most challenging people-related issue you've encountered in the last year? How did you handle it? What makes you happiest and most effective when working with others?

ONBOARDING TEMPLATE

TIMELINE	ACTIVITY	OWNER	DONE?
ONE MONTH TO ONE WEEK IN ADVANCE OF JOINING	Offer letter		
	Benefits overview		
	Send welcome letter		
	Assign required reading (if any)		
	Sign policies		
	Enter employee info into HR system		
	Order office or work area key; create ID card		
	Order business cards		
	Create email & send credentials		
	Grant access to any tools and create relevant accounts		
	Prepare benefits package		
	Discuss role, goals, and projects with supervisor/manager		
	Prepare employee's workstation (desk, phone, etc.)		
	Provide a job description		
	Welcome letter (start date and time, dress code, any additional info)		
	Welcome package (employee guide, important documents to read)		
	Team updates (if any changes since interviews)		
	Meeting invitations & list serves—forward recurring invitations and make sure employee is on appropriate list serves		

TIMELINE	ACTIVITY	OWNER	DONE?
FIRST DAY	Team welcome lunch		
	Assign a buddy; make sure new employee knows they can ask buddy any questions		
	Office tour		
	Give employee key/access card		
	Workstation—desk, equipment		
	Take out to lunch		
	Account setup/technology		
	Discuss role, goals, and projects with supervisor/manager		
	Debrief at end of day—any outstanding questions?		
FIRST WEEK	Introductions—introductory meetings/calls with key people—share list of key stakeholders in the organization		
	Team overview—review of org charts, who's who.		
	Review recent key deliverables and answer questions; share other background material (e.g., strategy decks)		
	Review existing projects		
	Assign first project (ideally first day)		
	Explain expectations for the first month		
	Plan check-in meetings/debriefs with manager		
	Assign a mentor		
	Team lunches—schedule lunches for the week		
	End-of-week debrief—answer outstanding questions		
FIRST MONTH	Employee creates individual development plan		
	Required training sessions and onboarding presentations (e.g., key clients, values)		
	Meeting with mentor		
	Meet for informal first-month performance check-in		
	Personalized long list of people that new person should meet / get to know		
	Collect feedback on onboarding process		

PSYCHOLOGICAL SAFETY TEAM ASSESSMENT

From: Edmondson, A. (1999). "Psychological safety and learning behavior in work teams." *Administrative Science Quarterly*, 44, 350–383.)

Psychological Safety represents the extent to which the team views the social climate as conducive to interpersonal risk; it is a measure of people's willingness to trust others not to attempt to gain personal advantage at their expense.

QUESTIONS TO ASSESS PSYCHOLOGICAL SAFETY ON A TEAM	1 "STRONGLY DISAGREE" 5 "STRONGLY AGREE"				
1. It is safe to take a risk on this team.	1	2	3	4	5
2. Members of this team are able to bring up problems and tough issues.	1	2	3	4	5
3. No one on this team would deliberately act in a way that undermines my efforts.	1	2	3	4	5
4. If you make a mistake on this team, it is often held against you.	1	2	3	4	5
5. People on this team sometimes reject others for being different.	1	2	3	4	5
6. It is difficult to ask other members of this team for help.	1	2	3	4	5
7. Working with members of this team, my unique skills and talents are valued and utilized.	1	2	3	4	5

TEAM NORMS TEMPLATE

What Kind of Team Are We?
Overall Approach to Team—Explicit Expectations & Objectives
What do we value?

Team Roles
(note taking, timekeeper, leader, building/sending agenda, synthesizer, etc.)
Do these roles change and how frequently?

Meeting Cadence & Schedule	**Meeting Structure & Tools** *(e.g., agendas)* *Delegation of tasks & follow-up*

How Do We Communicate?
- Mechanism (email, text, call)
- Response expectations

How Do We Hold Each Other Accountable?
(e.g., ways we give feedback)

Additional Norms

JOB DIMENSIONS

For each dimension, write down your preference and how important that preference is.

ORGANIZATION	
Size	
Stage (and Certainty)	
Industry	
For-Profit vs. Nonprofit	
Culture & Mission	

ROLE	
Function	
Skill Development	
Team & Management	
Title & Reporting	

LIFE NEEDS	
Geography	
Work/Life Balance	
Compensation—Pay	
Compensation—Other	
Commute & Travel	

NOTES

INTRODUCTION

1 Though the anecdotes sprinkled throughout this book reference actual events, names have been changed, shuffled, anonymized, disguised, and swapped. The one thing in common with all names is that they reference or imply a person who has been an integral part of the *Bringing Up the Boss* journey.

2 Throughout this book I use the pronouns *they/them/theirs* to reference an individual. I do this as an active choice to promote equity and inclusivity.

PART I: MANAGING AN INDIVIDUAL

CHAPTER 1: GREAT EXPECTATIONS

1 This quote is one of "Morgenstern's Maxims," written by the lawyer and venture capitalist Marc Morgenstern. You can find more of his gems of wisdom at www.bluemesapartners.com.

2 Justin Kruger and David Dunning, "Unskilled and Unaware of It: How Difficulties in Recognizing One's Own Incompetence Lead to Inflated Self-Assessments," *Journal of Personality and Social Psychology* 77, no. 6 (1999): 1121–1134.

CHAPTER 2: FEEDBACK IS LIKE UNDERWEAR: IT'S A GIFT YOU NEED, MAYBE NOT ONE YOU WANT

1 I'm not sure who originally developed this process, but it's been used for years to train folks on how to give and receive feedback.

2 C. Nathan DeWall and Brad J. Bushman, "Social acceptance and rejection: The sweet and the bitter," *Current Directions in Psychological Science* 20, no. 4 (2011): 256–260.

3 Ola Svenson, "Are we all less risky and more skillful than our fellow drivers?" *Acta Psychologica* 47, no. 2 (1981): 143–148.

4 Bernard Weiner, "An attributional theory of achievement motivation and emotion," *Psychological Review* 92, no. 4 (1985): 548.

5 This scale is adapted from: Marcus Buckingham and Ashley Goodall, "Reinventing Performance Management," *Harvard Business Review* 93, no. 4 (2015), 40–50.

CHAPTER 3: OWN IT! (YOUR DEVELOPMENT, THAT IS)

1 Edwin A. Locke and Gary. P. Latham, *A Theory of Goal Setting & Task Performance* (Englewood Cliffs, NJ: Prentice-Hall, 1990).

2 I built my first development plan template and broader development program with the incredible team at Sand Cherry Associates.

CHAPTER 4: THE COACHING PLAYBOOK

1 There is a long line of research about the importance of trust in relationships. Some of my favorite, seminal overviews include:

Mark Granovetter, "Economic action and social structure: The problem of embeddedness," *American Journal of Sociology* 91, no. 3 (1985), 481–510.

Peter M. Blau, "Social exchange," *International Encyclopedia of the Social Sciences 7* (1968), 452–457.

2 Another great reference for coaching questions is 31 Powerful Questions from *Co-Active Coaching*. The questions can be found at www.coactive .com.

CHAPTER 5: MANAGING PERFORMANCE ANXIETY

1 Besides being a professor at Harvard Business School, Chris Argyris was a thought leader at the Monitor Group, a consulting firm that was my first place of postcollegial employment and where I was first introduced to the ladder of inference. More on his ladder of inference can be found here: Peter M. Senge, *The Fifth Discipline: The Art and Practice of the Learning Organization* (New York: Broadway Business, 2006).

2 A powerful corollary of confirmation bias is the Matthew effect. The Matthew effect is the effect of accumulated advantage ("The rich get richer, the poor get poorer."). In organizations, we see the Matthew effect and the confirmation bias go hand-in-hand. Strong performers continue to be perceived as strong performers and continue to accumulate promotions, great projects, and accolades. A weaker performer may get stuck in a perennial hole and is never able to pull himself out once he is perceived as a weak performer, no matter how strong he becomes over time.

3 For legal reasons, a performance improvement plan also provides clear documentation that you and your organization sufficiently communicated performance issues for your team member and took reasonable steps to help your team member improve upon those performance issues.

A FINAL NOTE ON PERFORMANCE

1 A great summary of the flip-flopping nature of what works best for performance reviews can be found in these articles:

Marcus Buckingham and Ashley Goodall, "Reinventing Performance Management," *Harvard Business Review* 93, no. 4 (2015), 40–50.

Lori Goler, Janelle Gale, and Adam Grant, "Let's Not Kill Performance Evaluations Yet," *Harvard Business Review* 94, no. 11 (2016), 90–94.

2 One manager I know has a "performance diary" that he keeps year-round. It's a Word doc that is just a running list of performance notes for all of his team members. That way, at the end-of-the-year review period, he can quickly and easily pull up a whole bunch of specific examples of how his team performed. I like this idea, but only if the performance diary also includes a notation that shows whether or not the manager gave real-time feedback for each of the diary entries.

MOTIVATION

1 For those of you managers who are too young to remember, *Jock Jams* was a compilation of popular psych-up hits often played at the beginning of high school basketball games and other such endeavors. Select tunes included "Let's Get Ready to Rumble," "Tubthumping," and "Whoomp! (There It Is)."

CHAPTER 6: THE TRIFECTA OF MOTIVATION: ACHIEVEMENT, POWER, AND AFFILIATION

1 David C. McClelland, "Methods of measuring human motivation," *Motives in Fantasy, Action, and Society* (1958), 7–42.

2 The technical terms for the five love languages are words of affirmation, acts of service, receiving gifts, quality time, and physical touch. See: Gary D. Chapman, *The Five Love Languages: How to Express Heartfelt Commitment to Your Mate* (Chicago: Northfield Pub, 1995). Note that I often bemoan the fact that food isn't the sixth love language. Where does the theory of "the way to the heart is through the stomach" fit into Chapman's work?

CHAPTER 7: GOAL INTERRUPTED: THE GOOD AND THE BAD OF SETTING GOALS

1   The grandfathers of goal-setting theory are Edwin Locke and Gary Latham. They have hundreds of research studies on goals. A summary can be found here: Edwin A. Locke and Gary P. Latham, "Building a practically useful theory of goal setting and task motivation: A thirty-five-year odyssey," *American Psychology* 57, no. 9 (2002), 705.

2   If you want to discuss more about the negative side of setting goals, the best summary of goals as a dark art is: Lisa D. Ordóñez, Maurice E. Schweitzer, Adam D. Galinsky, and Max H. Bazerman, "Goals gone wild: The systematic side effects of overprescribing goal setting," *Academy of Management Perspectives* 23, no. 1 (2009), 6–16.

3   One of my favorite examples of goals driving the absolute wrong type of behavior can be found in an article about teachers doctoring students' state-wide exams in order to show better results: Rachel Aviv, "Wrong Answer," *New Yorker* 21 (2014), 54–65.

4   Emily Flitter, "The Price of Wells Fargo's Fake Account Scandal Grows by $3 Billion," *New York Times*, February 21, 2020.

5   Mike Isaac, "Uber Faces Federal Inquiry Over Use of Greyball Tool to Evade Authorities," *New York Times*, May 4, 2017.

6   Yoga Sutra 1.12: "Their suppression (is brought about) by persistent practice and non-attachment." See: Patañjali, *The Yoga Sutras of Patanjali: The Book of the Spiritual Man: An Interpretation* (London, UK: Watkins Publishing, 1975).

CHAPTER 8: THE COMPLICATIONS OF COMPENSATION

1   Edward L. Deci, "Effects of externally mediated rewards on intrinsic motivation," *Journal of Personality and Social Psychology* 18, no. 1 (1971), 105–115.

2 Daniel Kahneman, *Thinking, Fast and Slow* (New York: Macmillan, 2011).

3 J. Stacy Adams, "Inequity in social exchange," in *Advances in Experimental Social Psychology,* Vol. 2 (Cambridge, MA: Academic Press, 1965), 267–299.

4 Want to read more about procedural justice in the context of organizations? Tons of good stuff in: Chris Argyris, Robert Putnam, and Diana McLain Smith, *Action Science* (San Francisco, CA: Jossey-Bass, 1985).

CHAPTER 9: THE HEAVYWEIGHT TITLE FIGHT

1 Laurence J. Peter and Raymond Hull, *The Peter Principle: Why Things Always Go Wrong* (New York: William Morrow & Co., 1969).

A FINAL NOTE ON MOTIVATION

1 Edward Deci and Richard Ryan are the grandfathers of intrinsic motivation, self-determination theory, and learning. If you want to know more about how learning drives intrinsic motivation, they have a great (and detailed) handbook on all of these topics: Edward L. Deci and Richard M. Ryan, "Overview of self-determination theory: An organismic dialectical perspective," *Handbook of Self-Determination Research* (2002), 3–33.

2 Mr. Rogers said that "play is often talked about as if it were a relief from serious learning. But for children, play is serious learning."

3 Consulting firms often subscribe to a principle of creating a "slide a day." What this means in practice is at the end of the day, synthesize all that you learned during the day into a slide. It's a way of continually pushing along an idea or hypothesis, but also helps to build the muscle of synthesizing disparate pieces of information into something "usable" each day. Great to have your teams do this as well.

4 Job-rotation programs are an amazing way to do this as well, but they are often costly and difficult to implement, especially for small organizations. But if you can develop even a minijob rotation program where your team members can experience different roles and different functions, it's an amazing way for your team to learn and continue to grow. And research shows that individuals who develop broader expertise (e.g., are exposed to a whole bunch of different functions) are more likely to become senior executives later in their careers! Shinjae Won, a management professor at the University of Illinois, studies this phenomenon if you would like to read more research on this topic.

MEANING

1 Charles Duhigg, "America's Professional Elite: Wealthy, Successful, and Miserable," *New York Times Magazine* (2019).

2 My all-time favorite book for finding one's cosmic Meaning is *The Untethered Soul* by Mickey Singer. Life changing.

CHAPTER 10: MAKING WORK MEANINGFUL

1 J. Richard Hackman, Gary Oldham, Robert Janson, and Kenneth Purdy, "A new strategy for job enrichment," *California Management Review* 17, no. 4 (1975), 57–71.

2 Adam M. Grant, Elizabeth M. Campbell, Grace Chen, Keenan Cottone, David Lapedis, and Karen Lee, "Impact and the art of motivation maintenance: The effects of contact with beneficiaries on persistence behavior," *Organizational Behavior and Human Decision Processes* 103, no. 1 (2007), 53–67.

3 Amy Wrzesniewski, Justin M. Berg, and Jane E. Dutton, "Managing yourself: Turn the job you have into the job you want," *Harvard Business Review* 88, no. 6 (2010), 114–117.

CHAPTER 11: THERE'S NO CRYING IN BASEBALL

1   There is much research that discusses identity and emotions and how the two interact. Bobby Smith helpfully pointed this out to me in the first draft of this chapter.

2   In the last few years, the term *emotional labor* has been extended to include any type of unpaid work that different groups (most often women) are expected to do (e.g., organizing office events, helping a friend talk through a break-up, supporting a spouse's emotional needs). Of course, this emotional work is also an important dynamic at work that is necessary to be aware of and manage well; but for this chapter, I am using the original definition of emotional labor.

3   Interestingly, psychologists and sociologists talk about managing emotional labor through surface acting and deep acting. Surface acting occurs when the employee displays emotions that he is not actually feeling, whereas deep acting occurs when the employee actually works to change his emotional state to better align with the expectations and norms required by the job or the organization.

4   The impact of emotions at work is a well-studied and in-depth field. Past research shows that different emotions impact outcomes such as judgment and decision making, creativity, prosocial behavior (e.g., helping behavior), and risk-taking. For a detailed overview, see: Arthur P. Brief and Howard M. Weiss, "Organizational behavior: Affect in the workplace," *Annual Review of Psychology* 53, no. 1 (2002), 279–307.

5   Dr. Mark Hyman talks about this concept in his interview with former surgeon general Vivek Murthy. They were discussing the impact of loneliness, and how questions that go below the surface can help to combat that feeling of deep isolation. The podcast *Why Loneliness is a Public Health Issue* can be found at www.drhyman.com.

6   The concept that the workplace is a social system was first crystallized in the Hawthorne Studies. Any good student of psychology has heard

of the Hawthorne Effect—when research subjects change their behavior because they are being observed by researchers. What fewer students realize is that the power of the Hawthorne Studies—a research project in a Western Electric factory in the 1920s—lies in the finding that the workplace is a social system. And that the social dynamics of groups at work have a far greater impact on productivity than other incentives or punishments. We behave the way we do at work not because of bonuses or accolades, but because we want to align with group norms and not be shunned by our colleagues. We want to do a good job so that we don't let our team down, not because of some "punishment" that might be doled out. See: Elton Mayo, "Hawthorne and the Western Electric Company," *Public Administration: Concepts and Cases* (1949), 149–158.

CHAPTER 12: TALK IS NOT CHEAP

1 Unless, of course, your culture is built on radical transparency. For example, Bridgewater, a Connecticut-based hedge fund, prides itself on complete transparency. Every conversation and meeting in the company is recorded, and employees expect and understand that nothing is private.

2 Yaacov Trope and Nira Liberman, "Construal-level theory of psychological distance," *Psychological Review* 117, no. 2 (2010), 440.

3 Paul Slovic, David Zionts, Andrew K. Woods, Ryan Goodman, and Derek Jinks, "Psychic numbing and mass atrocity," *The Behavioral Foundations of Public Policy* (2013), 126–142.

CHAPTER 13: BEAUTIFUL QUESTIONS

1 Krista Tippett, "The Conversational Nature of Reality," *On Being*, April 6, 2017.

2 Daniel Ellsberg not only developed the term *ambiguity effect*—which you can read more about in his book: Daniel Ellsberg, *Risk, Ambiguity and Decision* (Routledge, 2015)—but also was the gentleman responsible for releasing the Pentagon Papers. A man of many talents.

3   For more information about the power of vulnerability and trust, check out the reigning queen on this topic, Brené Brown. A good place to start is her TED Talk: *The Power of Vulnerability.*

4   Perhaps the most famous example of this is Mandy Len Catron's article "To Fall in Love With Anyone, Do This," Modern Love, *New York Times,* January 9, 2015. This article was based on the academic research of Arthur Aron, Edward Melinat, Elaine N. Aron, Robert Darrin Vallone, and Renee J. Bator, "The experimental generation of interpersonal closeness: A procedure and some preliminary findings," *Personality and Social Psychology Bulletin* 23, no. 4 (1997), 363–377.

5   The full set of questions—as shared with me by my professional bioroboticist and amateur philosopher friend Zach—are the following: What is the single most important guiding principle that you live by? Both in theory, and in *practice?* That is, what are the primary needs, desires, and forces that drive your decisions and behaviors on a day-to-day and moment-to-moment basis? How much space is there between the *theory* and the *practice,* and how can you minimize this space?

6   There are lots of great resources for beautiful questions. Some of my favorite resources include Byron Katie's *The Work of Byron Katie,* The Baptiste Institute, and Jen Coken's blog www.jencoken.com.

7   This line of questioning is called "the miracle question." Therapists and coaches use it to help their clients paint a vivid picture of what the world would look like if the central challenge they are grappling with suddenly disappeared.

PART II: MANAGING A TEAM

CHAPTER 14: INTERVIEWING 101

1   Ann Marie Ryan and Nancy T. Tippins, "Attracting and selecting: What psychological research tells us," in "The Contributions of Psychologi-

cal Research to Human Resource Management," special issue, *Human Resource Management* 43, no. 4 (2004), 305–318. Published in cooperation with the School of Business Administration, The University of Michigan, and in alliance with the Society of Human Resources Management.

2   Powerful research by Marianne Bertrand and Sendil Mullainathan shows that hiring managers implicitly penalize job candidates with African American–sounding names: Marianne Bertrand and Sendil Mullainathan, "Are Emily and Greg more employable than Lakisha and Jamal? A field experiment on labor market discrimination," *American Economic Review* 94, no. 4 (2004), 991–1013.

CHAPTER 15: WHY THE AIRPORT TEST STINKS

1   Robert Sutton makes the case that yes, you do want to hire fundamentally good people in his book *The No Asshole Rule*. Robert I. Sutton, *The No Asshole Rule: Building a Civilized Workplace and Surviving One That Isn't* (New York: Business Plus, 2007).

2   I like to conduct an exercise with my team where we list the cultural values we want on our team (e.g., humility or grit or relationship-oriented), then we brainstorm a list of behavioral questions that could test those values. We hone the questions to get closer and closer to what we actually want to test.

CHAPTER 16: THE NEW KID ON THE BLOCK

1   Sociologists have long-studied in-groups and out-groups and the dynamics that result from them. The classic research that helped establish these findings of rivalry comes from the Robber's Cave Experiment, a 1950s experiment of two groups of boys at a summer camp in Oklahoma. The two groups hated each other for no other reason than the fact that they were part of two different groups. This experiment was the foundation for intergroup conflict theory. See: Muzafer Sherif, O. J. Harvey, Jack White, William R. Hood, and Carolyn W. Sherif, *The Robbers Cave Study: Intergroup Conflict and Cooperation* (Norman, OK: University Book Exchange, 1961).

2 Atul Gawande, *The Checklist Manifesto: How to Get Things Right* (New Delhi, India: Penguin Books India, 2010).

A FINAL NOTE ON HIRING AND FIRING

1 William Bridges, *Managing Transitions: Making the Most of Change* (Boston, MA: Da Capo Press, 2009).

2 Bridges based much of his framework on the transitions and emotions that happen after grief, as discussed in: Elizabeth Kübler-Ross, *On Death and Dying* (New York: Macmillan, 1969). Interestingly, this also means that many will not move through the emotions linearly and that people may "return" or cycle back to emotions that are at the beginning of the transition journey.

3 My favorite writings on uncertainty can be found in: Pema Chödrön, *When Things Fall Apart: Heart Advice for Difficult Times* (Boulder, CO: Shambhala Publications, 2000).

TEAM DYNAMICS

1 A Makarov pistol, for you non-gun aficionados out there, is a Soviet style semiautomatic pistol from the 1950s. It inspires little-to-no confidence from a safety perspective.

CHAPTER 18: THE TINO (TEAM IN NAME ONLY)

1 For a great summary of this research, see: Charles Duhigg, "What Google Learned From Its Quest to Build the Perfect Team," *New York Times*, February 25, 2016.

2 Amy Edmondson, "Psychological safety and learning behavior in work teams," *Administrative Science Quarterly* 44, no. 2 (1999), 350–383.

3   Want a fun way to see if you're high on the empathy scale? Take the eye test developed from research by Simon Baron-Cohen of the University of Cambridge which can be accessed at: https://well.blogs.nytimes.com/2013/10/03/well-quiz-the-mind-behind-the-eyes.

4   Google has a helpful spreadsheet of interventions you can take as a manager to build psychological safety into your team. You can find them at https://rework.withgoogle.com.

5   There are lots of people who are trained in interpreting the results of these assessments. Again, I like to use them as a safe jumping-off point for discussions and team building. The Gallup StrengthsFinder can be found at: https://www.gallup.com. The Enneagram Tool can be found at: https://www.enneagraminstitute.com.

CHAPTER 19: GETTING YOUR TEAM TO SPEAK UP

1   John Carreyrou, *Bad Blood: Secrets and Lies in a Silicon Valley Startup* (New York: Knopf, 2018).

2   Isaac, "Uber Faces Federal Inquiry Over Use of Greyball Tool to Evade Authorities."

3   Kenneth Jones and Tema Okun, "White Supremacy Culture," in *Dismantling Racism: A Workbook For Social Change Groups* (Changework, 2001).

4   Solomon Elliot Asch and Harold Guetzkow, "Effects of group pressure upon the modification and distortion of judgments," *Organizational Influence Processes* (1951), 295–303.

5   If you want to read more about what happens in terms of information flow and teams, check out Garold Stasser and W. Titus, "Pooling of unshared information in group decision making: Biased information sampling during discussion," *Journal of Personality and Social Psychology* 48,

no. 6 (1985), 1467. And: Gwen Wittenbaum and Jonathan M. Bowman, "A social validation explanation for mutual enhancement," *Journal of Experimental Social Psychology* 40, no. 2 (2004), 169–184.

6 Lots more good stuff in this article about raising the white flag on teams and how to prevent it from happening in the first place: Paul W. Mulvey, John F. Veiga, and Priscilla M. Elsass, "When teammates raise a white flag," *Academy of Management Perspectives* 10, no. 1 (1996), 40–49.

CHAPTER 20: THE GOOD FIGHT: CONFLICT AND WHAT TO DO ABOUT IT

1 There is so much fascinating research about conflict in teams. The three types of conflict and the patterns of conflict that high-performing teams exhibit are explored by Karen Jehn and Elizabeth Mannix. See: Karen A. Jehn and Elizabeth A. Mannix, "The Dynamic Nature of Conflict: A Longitudinal Study of Intragroup Conflict and Group Performance," *Academy of Management Journal* 44, no. 2 (2001), 238–251.

2 There are so many great nuggets in Gottlieb's book: Lori Gottlieb, *Maybe You Should Talk to Someone: A Therapist, HER Therapist, and Our Lives Revealed* (New York: Houghton Mifflin, 2019).

3 Jehn and Mannix, "The Dynamic Nature of Conflict."

CHAPTER 21: THE MEETING PARADOX: WE HATE GOING, BUT WE STILL WANT TO BE INVITED

1 This virtual meeting principle comes directly from LifeLabs Learning and their incredible guide to remote work. You can check it out at https://lifelabslearning.com.

A FINAL NOTE ON TEAM DYNAMICS

1 Some management scholars do talk about community as an additional perspective on the culture research. A great article about communities of practice as an organizational orientation can be found at: Etienne C. Wenger and William M. Snyder, "Communities of Practice: The Organizational Frontier," *Harvard Business Review* 78, no. 1 (2000), 139–146.

2 Sociologist Robert Putnam wrote about the demise of community and social structures in his seminal book that's definitely worth checking out if you want to read more about this topic. See: Robert D. Putnam, *Bowling Alone: The Collapse and Revival of American Community* (New York: Simon and Schuster, 2000).

PART III: MANAGING YOURSELF

1 Remarks by the President at "Hamilton at the White House," March 14, 2016, https://obamawhitehouse.archives.gov/the-press -office/2016/03/14/remarks-president-hamilton-white-house.

CHAPTER 22: CONFIDENCE AND VULNERABILITY

1 Apparently, according to the internet, Theodore Roosevelt is responsible for the second quote, and Maya Angelou, the third.

2 Defensiveness is a characteristic of oppressive cultures. According to the workbook *Dismantling Racism,* defensiveness comes about "because of either/or thinking, criticism of those with power is viewed as threatening and inappropriate (or rude); People respond to new or challenging ideas with defensiveness, making it very difficult to raise these ideas; A lot of energy in the organization is spent trying to make sure that people's feelings aren't getting hurt or working around defensive people; The defensiveness of people in power creates an oppressive culture." Furthermore, an additional characteristic is the Right to Comfort, "the

belief that those with power have a right to emotional and psychological comfort (another aspect of valuing logic over emotion)." Jones and Okun, "White Supremacy Culture."

CHAPTER 23: POWER: USE IT FOR GOOD, NOT EVIL

1 This phenomenon of wanting to maintain and hold power has long been studied by sociologists, political scientists, and psychologists. Additionally, it underpins much of the work required to dismantle racist and unjust systems and structures and build anti-oppressive organizations.

2 Kathleen M. Eisenhardt and L. J. Bourgeois III, "Politics of strategic decision making in high-velocity environments: Toward a midrange theory," *Academy of Management Journal* 31, no. 4 (1988), 737–770.

3 Adam D. Galinsky, Joe C. Magee, Deborah H. Gruenfeld, Jennifer A. Whitson, and Katie A. Liljenquist, "Power reduces the press of the situation: Implications for creativity, conformity, and dissonance," *Journal of Personality and Social Psychology* 95, no. 6 (2008), 1450–1466.

4 Elinor Amit and Joshua D. Greene, "You see, the ends don't justify the means: Visual imagery and moral judgment," *Psychological Science* 23, no. 8 (2012), 861–868.

CHAPTER 24: MANAGING UP

1 An Australian, John Sweller, developed Cognitive Load Theory, first written about in his PhD thesis: John Sweller, *Effects of Initial Discrimination Training on Subsequent Shift Learning in Animals and Humans* (doctoral dissertation, Adelaide, Australia, 1972).

2 Thomas Gilovich, Victoria H. Medvec, and Kenneth Savitsky, "The spotlight effect in social judgment: an egocentric bias in estimates of the salience of one's own actions and appearance," *Journal of Personality and Social Psychology* 78, no. 2 (2000), 211.

CHAPTER 25: SHOULD I STAY, OR SHOULD I GO?

1 Note that all start-ups when they are trying to recruit you are "fast-growing" and "well-funded." Whether that is actually the case is an entirely different story.

2 Mark Granovetter, *Getting a Job: A Study of Contacts and Careers* (Chicago, IL: University of Chicago Press, 2018).

3 Juno Demelo, "Precrastination: When the Early Bird Gets the Shaft," *New York Times*, March 25, 2019.

ACKNOWLEDGMENTS

In the spring of 2018, I met a friend in Baltimore for lunch. I shared with him my desire to write a book, and his immediate piece of advice was "Don't write a book. Start with a blog instead." From this advice, my blog was born, which led to the publication of this book. I share this story to recognize that so many people—friends, colleagues, clients, blog subscribers, family members, and students—have offered advice, encouragement, and countless other types of support big and small that made this book possible.

Instead of a standard acknowledgments page, the characters sprinkled throughout this book are named after all of you (or your children or, in a few instances, your dogs) who were instrumental in helping me along this book's journey. Your help may have been in the form of an encouraging email when I was ready to give up the slog of a weekly blog; it may have been in the form of suggesting a gnarly management topic that you were struggling with; it was in the form of taking a chance on a new author; it was the likes and reshares on social platforms; it was the grueling task of meticulously editing each chapter; it was letting me know when a blog was downright no good; and, it was the cheerleading to get this manuscript over the finish line.

To all of you, I say, thank you.

ABOUT THE ILLUSTRATIONS

I am often asked if I "drew" the figures throughout this book. I did not. Rather, to create the illustrations in each chapter, I embellished and adapted a set of figures from a wonderful resource called The Noun Project (www.thenounproject.com). The Noun Project is an organization that allows users to leverage a huge library of icons through a Creative Commons license, as well as purchase the use of adapted icons to support independent artists across the globe. Though I purchased the license to adapt the figures you see throughout this book, I wanted to bring attention to this awesome organization and the designers who created the figures, and to highlight the impact they are having on the world of graphic design and iconography.

The figures throughout the book were also chosen because of the level of detail that they offer the reader. Managers come in all ages, races, ethnicities, gender identities, and physical abilities, among many other characteristics. In wanting to acknowledge and honor all of these identities, I followed the guiding principles for inclusive, equitable, and diverse graphic design. In limiting identifying characteristics and portraying individuals in an abstract, stylized way, these illustrations aim to be inclusive of all.

All stick figures (except for below) created by Tatyana from Noun Project
Lion (page 31) created by Valerie Lamm from Noun Project
Unicorn (pages 133 and 242) created by Lauren Brajczewski from Noun Project

Butterfly (pages 133 and 242) created by Made x Made from Noun Project

Rainbow (pages 133 and 242) created by franc11s from Noun Project

Shooting star (pages 133 and 242) created by Aryadna Pons from Noun Project

Palm tree (page 134) created by starwin from Noun Project

Dog (page 247) created by Template from Noun Project

Company (pages 247) created by Alice Design from Noun Project

ABOUT THE AUTHOR

RACHEL PACHECO has long helped start-ups solve their people and culture challenges. She is on the board of advisors for numerous start-ups, primarily in the digital health and wellness space. Previously, she was on the executive teams of a health-care venture fund and advisory firm and a big data start-up incubated within JP Morgan Chase. Rachel has also lived and worked in Saudi Arabia, Dubai, Indonesia, and Kazakhstan, and thus has experienced the joy (and pain) of leading and managing organizations across many distinct cultures.

Rachel conducts research on management—specifically on power and conflict—at The Wharton School. She is a member of the founding faculty of the Entrepreneurship in Education Program at the University of Pennsylvania, where she teaches a popular Foundations in Management course to budding entrepreneurs and has developed numerous university courses that focus on the practical side of working in a small organization. She holds a PhD and MBA from The Wharton School and a BS from Georgetown University. Rachel resides in Washington, DC, with her husband, Michael.